THE AUSTRALIAN
Women's Weekly

How nice it is to be able to come home from work and cook an evening meal outside on the barbie in less than an hour. Long gone are the days of struggling to light coals then waiting ages to start cooking, so it seemed logical that we develop a book of recipes that match the barbecue in terms of simplicity and speed. *Barbecue Meals in Minutes* is exactly that, great weeknight dinner ideas that you can whip up in next to no time with a minimum of fuss and even less effort.

Pamela Clark

Food Director

contents

To Dad & Virginia
From our Xmas
to yours...
Something to
enjoy this summer.
Love from
Kate & Georgia
x x x
2004

beef

carpetbag steak en croûte

PREPARATION TIME 15 MINUTES **COOKING TIME** 25 MINUTES

12 oysters, on the half shell
4 beef eye fillet steaks (500g)
4 bacon rashers (280g), rind removed
2 small turkish breads (320g)
1 tablespoon olive oil
250g grape tomatoes
300g baby green beans

BALSAMIC VINAIGRETTE
2 tablespoons olive oil
¼ cup (60ml) balsamic vinegar
1 clove garlic, crushed
1 teaspoon dijon mustard

1 Remove oysters from shells. Using sharp knife, cut small pocket in
  side of each steak; insert three oysters in each pocket. Wrap one
  bacon rasher around each steak, trim to fit; secure with toothpicks.
2 Cook steaks on heated oiled grill plate, uncovered, until cooked
  as desired. Remove toothpicks.
3 Meanwhile, cut one 10cm round from each bread; split rounds in
  half. Brush with olive oil; toast bread both sides on heated flat plate.
4 Make balsamic vinaigrette.
5 Combine tomatoes and 2 tablespoons of the vinaigrette in small bowl.
  Cook tomatoes on heated oiled flat plate, uncovered, until just tender.
6 Meanwhile, boil, steam or microwave beans until just tender; drain.
7 Divide bread among serving plates; top with beans and steaks, serve
  with tomatoes, drizzle with remaining vinaigrette.

BALSAMIC VINAIGRETTE Place ingredients in screw-top jar;
shake well.

serves 4
per serving 31.3g fat; 2802kJ (669 cal)

fillet steak with marinated vegetable skewers

PREPARATION TIME 15 MINUTES **COOKING TIME** 15 MINUTES

You need eight bamboo skewers for this recipe. Soak them in cold water before using to prevent them from splintering and scorching.
Sliced char-grilled eggplant and capsicum are available at delicatessens.

1⅓ cups (200g) drained
   semi-dried tomatoes
50g butter, softened
175g char-grilled eggplant
   strips, halved lengthways
270g char-grilled capsicum
   strips, halved lengthways
4 beef eye fillet steaks (500g)
50g baby rocket leaves

1 Finely chop ⅓ cup of the tomato; combine with butter in small bowl. Place butter mixture on piece of plastic wrap; enclose butter mixture tightly in plastic wrap, shape into log. Refrigerate until required.
2 Thread eggplant, capsicum and remaining tomato, alternately, on skewers. Cook skewers on heated oiled grill plate, uncovered, until browned.
3 Meanwhile, cook steaks on heated oiled grill plate, uncovered, until cooked as desired.
4 Cut butter log into quarters. Divide steaks among serving plates; top each with butter. Serve with skewers and rocket.

serves 4
per serving 18.3g fat;
1649kJ (394 cal)

beef with green papaya, chilli and coriander salad

PREPARATION TIME 20 MINUTES **COOKING TIME** 15 MINUTES

600g piece beef rump steak

800g green papaya

2 medium tomatoes (300g),
    seeded, sliced thinly

3 cups (180g) finely shredded
    iceberg lettuce

2 lebanese cucumbers (260g),
    seeded, sliced thinly

⅓ cup (80ml) lime juice

2 tablespoons fish sauce

1 tablespoon brown sugar

2 cloves garlic, crushed

3 small green chillies, seeded,
    chopped finely

¼ cup coarsely chopped
    fresh coriander

1 Cook beef on heated oiled grill
   plate, uncovered, until cooked
   as desired. Cover beef; stand
   5 minutes, slice thinly.

2 Meanwhile, peel papaya.
   Quarter lengthways, discard
   seeds; grate papaya coarsely.

3 Place beef and papaya in large
   bowl with tomato, lettuce and
   cucumber. Place remaining
   ingredients in screw-top jar;
   shake well. Drizzle salad with
   dressing; toss gently to combine.

serves 4
per serving 10.5g fat;
1265kJ (302 cal)

fajitas with salsa cruda and avocado mash

PREPARATION TIME 25 MINUTES (PLUS REFRIGERATION TIME) **COOKING TIME** 15 MINUTES

2 tablespoons vegetable oil
⅓ cup (80ml) lime juice
¼ cup coarsely chopped fresh oregano
2 cloves garlic, crushed
¼ cup coarsely chopped fresh coriander
2 teaspoons ground cumin
800g beef skirt steak
1 medium red capsicum (200g), sliced thickly
1 medium green capsicum (200g), sliced thickly
1 medium yellow capsicum (200g), sliced thickly
1 large red onion (300g), sliced thickly
20 small flour tortillas

SALSA CRUDA
2 cloves garlic, crushed
3 medium tomatoes (450g), seeded, chopped finely
1 small white onion (80g), chopped finely
2 trimmed red radishes (30g), chopped finely
1 lebanese cucumber (130g), chopped finely
2 tablespoons coarsely chopped fresh coriander
1 fresh long red chilli, chopped finely
2 tablespoons lime juice

AVOCADO MASH
2 small avocados (400g)
2 tablespoons lime juice

1 Combine oil, juice, oregano, garlic, coriander and cumin in large bowl, add beef; toss beef to coat in marinade. Cover; refrigerate overnight.

2 Cook beef, capsicums and onion on heated oiled flat plate, uncovered, until beef is cooked as desired and vegetables are just tender. Cover to keep warm.

3 Meanwhile, make salsa cruda and avocado mash. Make four foil parcels of five tortillas each; heat parcels both sides on flat plate until tortillas are warm and just softened.

4 Cut beef into 1cm slices; combine with cooked vegetables in large bowl. Serve with salsa cruda, avocado mash and tortillas.

SALSA CRUDA Combine ingredients in small bowl.
AVOCADO MASH Mash avocado and juice in small bowl.

serves 4
per serving 33.5g fat; 3327kJ (795 cal)

sausages with caramelised onions, roasted kipflers and mushrooms

PREPARATION TIME 10 MINUTES **COOKING TIME** 25 MINUTES

Swiss brown mushrooms, also known as roman or cremini, are light- to dark-brown in colour and full-bodied in flavour.

750g kipfler potatoes
olive-oil cooking spray
¼ cup coarsely chopped
    fresh chives
200g swiss brown mushrooms,
    sliced thickly
8 thick beef sausages (640g)
2 large red onions (600g),
    sliced thinly
1 tablespoon balsamic vinegar
1 tablespoon brown sugar

1 Boil, steam or microwave potatoes until just tender; drain. Place on heated oiled flat plate; spray with oil. Cook potatoes, uncovered, until crisp. Remove from heat; sprinkle with chives.

2 Meanwhile, cook mushrooms and sausages on heated oiled flat plate, uncovered, until mushrooms are browned and sausages are cooked through.

3 Cook onion, stirring, on heated oiled flat plate until soft. Sprinkle with vinegar and sugar; cook, stirring, until onion is caramelised.

4 Divide potatoes, sausages and mushrooms among serving plates; top with onion mixture.

serves 4
per serving 41.8g fat;
2615kJ (625 cal)

veal with salsa verde and potato rösti

PREPARATION TIME 20 MINUTES **COOKING TIME** 15 MINUTES

800g piece veal tenderloin,
    halved lengthways
4 medium potatoes (800g)
1 egg

SALSA VERDE
⅔ cup finely chopped fresh
    flat-leaf parsley
⅓ cup finely chopped
    fresh mint
⅓ cup finely chopped fresh dill
⅓ cup finely chopped
    fresh chives
1 tablespoon wholegrain
    mustard
¼ cup (60ml) lemon juice
¼ cup (50g) drained baby
    capers, rinsed
2 cloves garlic, crushed
½ cup (125ml) olive oil

1 Make salsa verde.
2 Rub veal with half of the salsa
   verde; cook veal on heated
   oiled flat plate, uncovered, until
   cooked as desired. Cover veal;
   stand 5 minutes, slice thickly.
3 Meanwhile, grate potatoes
   coarsely. Using hands, squeeze
   excess moisture from potato.
   Combine potato and egg in
   medium bowl; divide into eight
   portions. Cook rösti portions on
   heated oiled flat plate, flattening
   with spatula, until browned both
   sides. Drain on absorbent paper.
4 Serve veal with rösti and
   remaining salsa verde.

SALSA VERDE Combine
ingredients in medium bowl.

serves 4
per serving 33.1g fat;
2531kJ (605 cal)

grilled cheesy polenta triangles with new york steaks

PREPARATION TIME 10 MINUTES (PLUS REFRIGERATION TIME) **COOKING TIME** 25 MINUTES

1 litre (4 cups) water
1 cup (170g) polenta
20g butter
100g provolone cheese, chopped finely
2 tablespoons red wine vinegar
⅓ cup (80ml) dry red wine
1 clove garlic, crushed
4 new york-cut steaks (880g)

ROCKET SALAD
¼ cup (60ml) olive oil
2 tablespoons red wine vinegar
1 tablespoon wholegrain mustard
1 teaspoon sugar
100g baby rocket leaves

1 Oil 19cm x 29cm slice pan.
2 Place the water in large saucepan; bring to a boil. Gradually add polenta to liquid, stirring constantly. Reduce heat; cook, stirring, about 10 minutes or until polenta thickens. Stir in butter and cheese then spread polenta into prepared pan; cool 10 minutes. Cover; refrigerate overnight.
3 Combine vinegar, wine and garlic in large bowl, add steaks; toss steaks to coat in marinade. Cover; refrigerate overnight.
4 Turn polenta onto board; trim edges. Cut polenta into six squares; cut each square in half diagonally to form two triangles. Cook polenta triangles on heated oiled grill plate, uncovered, until heated through. Cover to keep warm.
5 Meanwhile, cook drained steaks on heated oiled grill plate, uncovered, until cooked as desired.
6 Make rocket salad. Serve steaks with salad and polenta triangles; drizzle steaks with reserved dressing.

ROCKET SALAD Place oil, vinegar, mustard and sugar in screw-top jar; shake well. Place rocket and half of the dressing in large bowl; toss gently to combine. Reserve remaining dressing.

serves 4
per serving 40.3g fat; 3117kJ (745 cal)

TIP Make sure the grill plate is well oiled to prevent the polenta from sticking.

beef burger with blue-cheese mayonnaise on rye

PREPARATION TIME 15 MINUTES **COOKING TIME** 30 MINUTES

700g beef mince

1 medium brown onion (150g),
   chopped finely

2 tablespoons coarsely chopped fresh
   flat-leaf parsley

2 tablespoons coarsely chopped
   fresh oregano

¼ cup (15g) stale breadcrumbs

1 small kumara (250g), sliced thinly

6 slices prosciutto (90g)

12 slices rye bread

50g rocket leaves

2 medium tomatoes (300g), sliced thinly

BLUE-CHEESE MAYONNAISE

2 tablespoons finely chopped
   fresh chives

25g blue cheese, crumbled

¼ cup (75g) mayonnaise

2 tablespoons sour cream

1 Using hand, combine mince, onion, herbs and breadcrumbs in large bowl; shape mixture into six burgers. Cook burgers on heated oiled flat plate, uncovered, until cooked through. Cover to keep warm.

2 Meanwhile, cook kumara on heated oiled grill plate, uncovered, until tender. Cover to keep warm.

3 Make blue-cheese mayonnaise.

4 Cook prosciutto on heated oiled flat plate, uncovered, until crisp. Toast bread both sides on heated flat plate.

5 Divide kumara, tomato, prosciutto, burgers, mayonnaise and rocket among six bread slices; serve with remaining bread slices.

BLUE-CHEESE MAYONNAISE Combine ingredients in small bowl.

serves 6
per serving 19.6g fat; 2216kJ (529 cal)

beef and reef with kumara hash browns

PREPARATION TIME 20 MINUTES **COOKING TIME** 20 MINUTES

1 large kumara (500g),
    chopped coarsely
1 small brown onion (80g),
    chopped finely
2 tablespoons finely chopped
    fresh chives
1 egg yolk
16 uncooked medium king
    prawns (720g)
1 teaspoon salt
½ teaspoon cracked black pepper
½ teaspoon hot paprika
2 trimmed corn cobs (500g)
4 beef scotch fillet steaks (600g)

GARLIC BUTTER
50g butter, softened
2 cloves garlic, crushed
1 tablespoon finely chopped
    fresh chives

1 Boil, steam or microwave kumara until tender; drain. Mash kumara in medium bowl with onion, chives and egg yolk.

2 Meanwhile, shell and devein prawns, leaving tails intact. Combine salt, pepper and paprika in large bowl, add prawns; toss prawns to coat in mixture.

3 Cut corn in half crossways then in half lengthways. Cook steaks and corn on heated oiled grill plate, uncovered, until steaks are cooked as desired and corn is tender. Cover to keep warm.

4 Meanwhile, shape kumara mixture into four patties. Cook kumara patties on heated oiled flat plate, flattening with spatula, until browned both sides.

5 Make garlic butter.

6 Cook prawns on heated oiled grill plate, uncovered, until changed in colour.

7 Divide steaks among serving plates; top with prawns and butter. Serve with corn and hash browns.

GARLIC BUTTER Combine ingredients in small bowl.

serves 4
per serving 22.3g fat; 2339kJ (558 cal)

spiced steaks with dhal

PREPARATION TIME 10 MINUTES **COOKING TIME** 35 MINUTES

1½ teaspoons ground cumin

1 tablespoon ground coriander

2 teaspoons hot paprika

2cm piece fresh ginger (10g), grated

2 tablespoons vegetable oil

1kg beef rump steaks

1 lime, cut into wedges

⅔ cup loosely packed fresh coriander leaves

DHAL

1 tablespoon vegetable oil

1 medium brown onion (150g), chopped finely

4 cloves garlic, crushed

1cm piece fresh ginger (5g), grated

1 teaspoon ground cumin

1 teaspoon ground turmeric

1 litre (4 cups) water

2 medium tomatoes (300g), chopped coarsely

1½ cups (300g) red lentils

¼ cup coarsely chopped fresh coriander

1 Make dhal.

2 Meanwhile, combine spices, ginger and oil in large bowl, add steaks; toss steaks to coat in mixture.

3 Cook steaks on heated oiled grill plate, uncovered, until cooked as desired. Cover steaks; stand 5 minutes, slice thickly. Serve steak with dhal, lime and coriander leaves.

DHAL Heat oil in large heavy-based saucepan; cook onion, garlic and ginger, stirring, until onion softens. Stir in spices; cook, stirring, until fragrant. Add the water, tomato and lentils; bring to a boil. Reduce heat; simmer, uncovered, about 30 minutes or until lentils are tender, stirring occasionally. Stir in coriander.

serves 4

per serving 32.3g fat; 3005kJ (718 cal)

calves liver with onion, apple and potato wedges

PREPARATION TIME 10 MINUTES **COOKING TIME** 30 MINUTES

Calves liver should be sliced into paper-thin slices then quickly seared – overcooking toughens its delicate texture. Ask your butcher to slice the liver thinly for you.

5 small potatoes (600g),
    cut into wedges
¼ cup (35g) plain flour
1 teaspoon salt
1 teaspoon cracked
    black pepper
600g calves liver, sliced thinly
1 large red onion (300g),
    sliced thickly
1 large apple (200g),
    sliced thickly
500g asparagus, trimmed

1 Cook unpeeled potato on heated oiled grill plate, uncovered, about 20 minutes or until tender.
2 Meanwhile, combine flour, salt and pepper in shallow medium bowl. Coat liver in flour mixture; place, in single layer, on tray.
3 Cook onion and apple on heated oiled grill plate, uncovered, until tender and lightly browned.
4 Meanwhile, cook asparagus on heated oiled flat plate, uncovered, until just tender.
5 Cook liver on heated oiled flat plate, uncovered, about 1 minute or until cooked as desired. Serve liver with potato, onion, apple and asparagus.

serves 4
per serving 13.3g fat;
1760kJ (421 cal)

mustard and thyme T-bone steaks with honey sweet potato and kumara

PREPARATION TIME 10 MINUTES (PLUS REFRIGERATION TIME) **COOKING TIME** 30 MINUTES

2 tablespoons dijon mustard
1 tablespoon fresh
  thyme leaves
2 tablespoons olive oil
4 T-bone steaks (1.2kg)
700g kumara, sliced thickly
700g white sweet potatoes,
  sliced thickly
1 tablespoon hot water
¼ cup (90g) honey
1 cup firmly packed fresh
  flat-leaf parsley leaves

1 Combine mustard, thyme and half of the oil in small bowl. Rub mustard mixture into steaks. Cover; refrigerate overnight.
2 Boil, steam or microwave kumara and potato until just tender; drain.
3 Combine the water, honey and remaining oil in small bowl. Cook kumara and potato on heated oiled grill plate, uncovered, brushing with honey mixture, until golden brown.
4 Cook steaks on heated oiled grill plate, uncovered, until cooked as desired.
5 Sprinkle kumara and potato with parsley; serve with steaks.

serves 4
per serving 21g fat;
2577kJ (615 cal)

spicy beef, cucumber and witlof salad

PREPARATION TIME 15 MINUTES **COOKING TIME** 20 MINUTES

Sometimes spelled witloof, and in some countries known as belgian endive or chicory, witlof is a versatile vegetable, and tastes as good cooked as it does raw. You need about a quarter of a medium chinese cabbage for this recipe.

2 teaspoons ground cumin
1 teaspoon ground coriander
1 teaspoon ground turmeric
1 teaspoon sweet paprika
1 teaspoon dried chilli flakes
800g piece beef eye fillet, halved lengthways
3 lebanese cucumbers (390g)
1 witlof (125g), trimmed
1¼ cups (100g) bean sprouts
100g snow pea sprouts
3 cups (240g) finely shredded chinese cabbage
4 green onions, sliced thinly
⅔ cup loosely packed fresh coriander leaves

SESAME AND LEMON VINAIGRETTE
⅓ cup (80ml) peanut oil
1 teaspoon sesame oil
2 tablespoons lemon juice
2 tablespoons white wine vinegar
2 teaspoons sugar
2 cloves garlic, crushed

1 Combine spices in small bowl; rub spice mixture into beef. Cook beef on heated oiled grill plate, covered, until cooked as desired. Cover beef; stand 5 minutes, slice thinly.
2 Meanwhile, make sesame and lemon vinaigrette.
3 Using vegetable peeler, cut cucumbers into ribbons. Cut witlof into quarters lengthways; separate leaves. Place cucumber and witlof in large bowl with sprouts, cabbage, onion and coriander.
4 Add beef to salad with dressing; toss gently to combine.

SESAME AND LEMON VINAIGRETTE Place ingredients in screw-top jar; shake well.

serves 6
per serving 21.9g fat; 1445kJ (345 cal)

veal cutlets with brussels sprouts and celeriac mash

PREPARATION TIME 10 MINUTES **COOKING TIME** 20 MINUTES

2 large potatoes (600g),
  chopped coarsely
500g celeriac, chopped
  coarsely
1 cup (250ml) buttermilk,
  warmed
4 veal chops (800g)
300g brussels sprouts, halved
20g butter, melted
2 teaspoons finely chopped
  fresh thyme
2 tablespoons lemon juice

1 Boil, steam or microwave
   potato and celeriac, separately,
   until tender; drain. Mash with
   buttermilk in large bowl until
   smooth. Cover to keep warm.
2 Meanwhile, cook veal on heated
   oiled grill plate, uncovered, until
   cooked as desired.
3 Cook sprouts on heated oiled flat
   plate, uncovered, until browned.
   Combine sprouts in medium bowl
   with butter, thyme and juice. Serve
   veal with mash and sprouts.

serves 4
per serving 9.8g fat;
1506kJ (360 cal)

mini asian-flavoured meatloaves with grilled vegetables

PREPARATION TIME 15 MINUTES **COOKING TIME** 25 MINUTES

1 tablespoon soy sauce

⅓ cup (80ml) char sui sauce

600g beef mince

4 green onions, sliced thinly

2 cloves garlic, crushed

190g can sliced water chestnuts, drained, chopped finely

1 fresh small red thai chilli, chopped finely

¼ cup (25g) packaged breadcrumbs

1 egg

1 large carrot (180g)

300g baby corn cobs

200g baby green beans

1 teaspoon sesame oil

¼ cup (60ml) soy sauce, extra

1 Combine soy sauce and char sui in small bowl. Using hand, combine beef, onion, garlic, chestnut, chilli, breadcrumbs, egg and 1 tablespoon of the char sui mixture in large bowl; shape mince mixture into four rectangular meatloaves. Wrap each meatloaf in lightly oiled foil; cook on heated flat plate, uncovered, turning occasionally, 15 minutes.

2 Remove foil; brush meatloaves with remaining char sui mixture. Cook on heated oiled flat plate, turning, until browned all over and cooked through.

3 Meanwhile, cut carrot into 6cm pieces. Cut pieces lengthways into thick slices, cut slices into thick strips. Divide carrot, corn and beans among four lightly oiled 15cm-square pieces of foil, sprinkle with combined oil and extra soy sauce; wrap foil around vegetables. Cook on heated flat plate, uncovered, about 8 minutes or until vegetables are just tender. Serve sliced meatloaves with vegetables.

serves 4
per serving 15.4g fat; 1685kJ (403 cal)

SERVING SUGGESTION Sprinkle meatloaves with thinly sliced green onion and serve with small bowls of sweet chilli sauce.

kofta with tunisian carrot salad

PREPARATION TIME 15 MINUTES **COOKING TIME** 15 MINUTES

500g lamb mince
1 cup (70g) fresh breadcrumbs
¼ cup finely chopped fresh mint
1 teaspoon ground allspice
1 teaspoon ground coriander
1 teaspoon cracked black pepper
1 tablespoon lemon juice
200g yogurt

TUNISIAN CARROT SALAD
3 large carrots (540g)
¼ cup (60ml) lemon juice
1 tablespoon olive oil
½ teaspoon ground cinnamon
½ teaspoon ground coriander
¼ cup firmly packed fresh mint leaves
¼ cup (35g) roasted shelled pistachios
¼ cup (40g) sultanas

1 Using hand, combine mince, breadcrumbs, mint, spices and juice in medium bowl; roll mixture into 12 balls, roll balls into sausage-shaped kofta. Cook kofta on heated oiled flat plate, uncovered, until cooked through.
2 Meanwhile, make tunisian carrot salad.
3 Serve kofta with salad and yogurt.

TUNISIAN CARROT SALAD Cut carrot into 5cm pieces; slice pieces thinly lengthways. Cook carrot on heated oiled grill plate, uncovered, until just tender. Place carrot in large bowl with remaining ingredients; toss gently to combine.

serves 4
per serving 20g fat; 1844kJ (441 cal)

grilled backstraps with broad bean and beetroot salad

PREPARATION TIME 15 MINUTES **COOKING TIME** 15 MINUTES

2 cups (300g) frozen
  broad beans
450g can baby beetroots,
  drained, quartered
60g rocket leaves
4 lamb backstraps (800g)

ANCHOVY DRESSING
6 drained anchovy fillets,
  chopped finely
1 tablespoon drained
  baby capers, rinsed,
  chopped finely
2 tablespoons olive oil
2 teaspoons finely grated
  lemon rind
1 teaspoon dijon mustard
1 tablespoon red wine vinegar

1 Boil, steam or microwave beans until tender; drain. Peel away grey-coloured outer shells; place beans in large bowl with beetroot and rocket.

2 Meanwhile, make anchovy dressing. Add 2 tablespoons of the dressing to bowl with salad; toss gently to combine.

3 Cook lamb on heated oiled grill plate, uncovered, brushing occasionally with remaining dressing, until cooked as desired. Serve lamb with salad.

ANCHOVY DRESSING
Combine ingredients in small bowl.

serves 4
per serving 17.3g fat;
1743kJ (416 cal)

chops marinated in port, garlic and mustard with minted pea mash

PREPARATION TIME 10 MINUTES (PLUS REFRIGERATION TIME) **COOKING TIME** 20 MINUTES

½ cup (125ml) port
2 tablespoons wholegrain
  mustard
2 cloves garlic, crushed
8 lamb loin chops (800g)
¼ cup (60ml) cream

MINTED PEA MASH
600g potatoes
1¾ cups (210g) frozen peas
20g butter, melted
½ cup (125ml) milk, warmed
1 tablespoon finely chopped
  fresh mint

1 Combine port, mustard and
   garlic in large bowl, add lamb;
   toss lamb to coat in marinade.
   Cover; refrigerate overnight.
2 Make minted pea mash.
3 Meanwhile, drain lamb; reserve
   marinade. Cook lamb on heated
   oiled flat plate, uncovered, until
   cooked as desired.
4 Combine reserved marinade and
   cream in small saucepan; bring
   to a boil. Reduce heat; simmer,
   about 3 minutes or until sauce
   thickens slightly. Serve lamb with
   mash, drizzled with sauce.

MINTED PEA MASH Boil,
steam or microwave potatoes
and peas, separately, until just
tender; drain. Mash potato in
large bowl with butter and milk.
Using fork, crush peas lightly in
small bowl; stir peas and mint
into mash.

serves 4
per serving 24.2g fat;
2173kJ (519 cal)

za'atar-crusted kebabs with hummus

PREPARATION TIME 20 MINUTES **COOKING TIME** 15 MINUTES

Za'atar is a Middle-Eastern blend of roasted dried spices; you can make your own as shown below or you can purchase it ready-made from Middle-Eastern food stores. You need eight bamboo skewers for this recipe; soak them in cold water before use to prevent them from splintering or scorching.

1 tablespoon olive oil
1 tablespoon lemon juice
800g diced lamb
½ cup coarsely chopped fresh flat-leaf parsley
8 pieces lavash
200g yogurt

HUMMUS
2 x 300g cans chickpeas, rinsed, drained
1 clove garlic, quartered
½ cup (140g) tahini
½ cup (125ml) lemon juice
½ cup (125ml) water

ZA'ATAR
1 tablespoon sumac
1 tablespoon toasted sesame seeds
1 teaspoon dried marjoram
2 teaspoons dried thyme

1 Combine oil and juice in medium bowl, add lamb; toss lamb to coat in mixture. Thread lamb onto skewers.
2 Make hummus. Cover; refrigerate until required.
3 Make za'atar; spread on tray. Roll kebabs in za'atar until coated all over. Cook kebabs on heated oiled grill plate, uncovered, until cooked as desired. Serve kebabs on lavash with hummus, parsley and yogurt.

HUMMUS Blend or process ingredients until smooth.
ZA'ATAR Combine ingredients in small bowl.

serves 4
per serving 51g fat; 4599kJ (1099 cal)

meatballs with pasta, tomato and red onion

PREPARATION TIME 15 MINUTES **COOKING TIME** 20 MINUTES

800g lamb mince
1 egg
½ cup (40g) finely grated
   parmesan cheese
½ cup (35g) stale breadcrumbs
¼ cup finely chopped fresh
   flat-leaf parsley
½ cup finely chopped
   fresh basil
6 large egg tomatoes (540g),
   cut into wedges
1 medium red onion (170g),
   cut into wedges
375g large spiral pasta
¾ cup loosely packed fresh
   basil leaves, torn
¼ cup (60ml) olive oil

1 Using hand, combine mince, egg,
   cheese, breadcrumbs, parsley
   and chopped basil in large bowl;
   roll mixture into 16 balls. Cook
   meatballs on heated oiled flat plate,
   uncovered, until cooked through.
2 Cook tomato and onion on heated
   oiled flat plate, uncovered, until
   onion softens.
3 Meanwhile, cook pasta in large
   saucepan of boiling water,
   uncovered, until just tender; drain.
4 Place tomato, onion and pasta in
   large bowl with torn basil leaves
   and oil; toss gently to combine.
   Divide pasta among serving bowls;
   top with meatballs and flaked
   parmesan cheese, if desired.

serves 4
per serving 34.5g fat;
3578kJ (855 cal)

lamb fillets in sumac with chickpea salad

PREPARATION TIME 10 MINUTES **COOKING TIME** 10 MINUTES

1 tablespoon sumac

8 lamb fillets (800g)

1 cup (120g) frozen peas

2 x 300g cans chickpeas,
   rinsed, drained

1 medium red capsicum (200g),
   chopped finely

1 small red onion (80g),
   chopped finely

CITRUS DRESSING
½ cup (125ml) orange juice
¼ cup (60ml) lemon juice
2 tablespoons olive oil

1 Make citrus dressing. Combine sumac and 2 tablespoons of the dressing in medium bowl, add lamb; toss lamb to coat in mixture.

2 Cook lamb on heated oiled grill plate, uncovered, until cooked as desired. Cover lamb; stand 5 minutes, slice diagonally.

3 Meanwhile, boil, steam or microwave peas until just tender; drain.

4 Place peas in large bowl with chickpeas, capsicum, onion and ½ cup of the remaining dressing; toss gently to combine. Serve lamb on salad; drizzle with remaining dressing.

CITRUS DRESSING Place ingredients in screw-top jar; shake well.

serves 4
per serving 29g fat;
2289kJ (547 cal)

harissa lamb cutlets with grilled corn and garlic

PREPARATION TIME 15 MINUTES (PLUS REFRIGERATION TIME) **COOKING TIME** 15 MINUTES

¼ cup (75g) harissa
2 tablespoons olive oil
12 lamb cutlets (900g)
4 fresh corn cobs (1.5kg), husks on
4 bulbs garlic

HARISSA BUTTER
3 teaspoons harissa
80g butter, softened

1   Combine harissa and oil in large bowl, add lamb; toss lamb to coat in marinade. Cover; refrigerate overnight.
2   Carefully pull husk down corn cob, leaving it attached at base. Remove as much silk as possible then bring husk back over cob to cover kernels. Tie each cob with kitchen string to hold husk in place; soak corn overnight in large bowl of water.
3   Make harissa butter. Spread 2 teaspoons of the harissa butter over each garlic bulb; wrap garlic bulbs individually in foil.
4   Drain corn. Cook corn and garlic parcels on heated oiled grill plate, uncovered, about 15 minutes or until corn is cooked as desired and garlic is tender.
5   Meanwhile, cook lamb on heated oiled grill plate, uncovered, until cooked as desired. Spread corn with remaining harissa butter; serve with lamb and garlic.

HARISSA BUTTER   Combine ingredients in small bowl.

serves 4
per serving 50.4g fat; 3565kJ (852 cal)

honey and soy lamb chops with grilled vegetables

PREPARATION TIME 10 MINUTES (PLUS REFRIGERATION TIME) **COOKING TIME** 15 MINUTES

½ cup (180g) honey
⅓ cup (80ml) soy sauce
8 lamb chump chops (880g)
6 baby eggplants (360g),
   halved lengthways
4 small green zucchini (360g),
   halved lengthways
1 large red onion (300g),
   cut into wedges

RED WINE VINAIGRETTE
2 cloves garlic, chopped finely
2 tablespoons olive oil
2 tablespoons red wine vinegar

1 Combine honey and soy sauce
   in large bowl, add lamb; toss
   lamb to coat in marinade. Cover;
   refrigerate overnight.
2 Make red wine vinaigrette.
3 Cook vegetables on heated oiled
   grill plate, uncovered, until tender.
   Place vegetables in large bowl
   with vinaigrette; toss gently to
   combine. Cover to keep warm.
4 Drain lamb; reserve marinade.
   Cook lamb on heated oiled
   grill plate, uncovered, brushing
   with reserved marinade, until
   cooked as desired. Serve
   lamb with vegetables.

RED WINE VINAIGRETTE
Place ingredients in screw-top
jar; shake well.

serves 4
per serving 34.7g fat;
2611kJ (624 cal)

lamb in lettuce cups

PREPARATION TIME 20 MINUTES **COOKING TIME** 20 MINUTES

2 teaspoons ground cumin

2 tablespoons sesame oil

2 cloves garlic, crushed

600g lamb strips

1 cup (200g) white
    long-grain rice

⅔ cup (160ml) teriyaki marinade

2 tablespoons sweet
    chilli sauce

1 telegraph cucumber (400g),
    seeded

3 fresh small red thai chillies,
    sliced thinly

4 green onions, sliced thinly

1 large butter lettuce,
    leaves separated

1 tablespoon toasted
    sesame seeds

1 Combine cumin, oil and garlic in
   medium bowl, add lamb; toss
   lamb to coat in mixture.

2 Cook rice in medium saucepan
   of boiling water, uncovered, until
   just tender; drain.

3 Meanwhile, combine teriyaki
   and sauce in small bowl. Cut
   cucumber into 8cm pieces; cut
   pieces lengthways into thick
   slices, cut slices lengthways into
   thick strips.

4 Cook lamb on heated oiled flat
   plate, uncovered, until cooked
   as desired.

5 Divide rice, cucumber, chilli,
   onion and lettuce leaves among
   serving plates; fill lettuce leaves
   with lamb mixture, sprinkle with
   sesame seeds. Serve with
   teriyaki mixture.

serves 4
per serving 16.6g fat;
2099kJ (501 cal)

lamb cutlets with mustard and basil cream

PREPARATION TIME 10 MINUTES **COOKING TIME** 20 MINUTES

600g kipfler potatoes, halved lengthways
1 teaspoon cracked black pepper
1 tablespoon olive oil
½ small red cabbage (600g), cut into four wedges
12 frenched lamb cutlets (1kg)

MUSTARD AND BASIL CREAM
2 teaspoons olive oil
1 clove garlic, crushed
¼ cup (60ml) dry white wine
300ml cream
1 tablespoon dijon mustard
¼ cup coarsely chopped fresh basil

1 Place potato in large bowl with pepper and oil; toss potato to coat in mixture. Cook potato, cabbage and lamb on heated oiled grill plate, uncovered, until potato and cabbage are tender and lamb cooked as desired. Cover to keep warm.
2 Meanwhile, make mustard and basil cream.
3 Serve lamb with cabbage and potato, drizzled with warm cream.

MUSTARD AND BASIL CREAM Heat oil in small frying pan; cook garlic, stirring, until fragrant. Add wine; bring to a boil. Reduce heat; simmer, uncovered, until liquid reduces by half. Add cream and mustard; cook, stirring, until sauce thickens slightly. Remove from heat; stir in basil.

serves 4
per serving 54.1g fat; 2918kJ (697 cal)

italian mixed grill

PREPARATION TIME 15 MINUTES **COOKING TIME** 20 MINUTES

Ask your butcher to slice the lamb liver thinly for you. Liver should be cooked
quickly as overcooking toughens its delicate texture.

4 frenched lamb cutlets (300g)
3 lamb fillets (300g)
1 teaspoon cracked black pepper
2 tablespoons olive oil
4 thin lamb sausages (320g)
4 small egg tomatoes (240g), halved
4 medium flat mushrooms (320g)
4 baby eggplants (320g),
  halved lengthways
8 baby brown onions (200g), halved
2 cloves garlic, crushed
200g piece lamb liver, sliced thinly
2 tablespoons plain flour
2 tablespoons balsamic vinegar
1 tablespoon fresh oregano leaves

1 Place cutlets and fillets in large bowl with pepper and half of the oil; toss cutlets and fillets to coat in mixture. Cook cutlets, fillets and sausages on heated oiled grill plate, uncovered, until cooked as desired. Cover to keep warm.

2 Combine tomato, mushrooms, eggplant, onion and garlic with remaining oil in large bowl. Cook vegetables on heated grill plate, uncovered, until browned lightly and just tender.

3 Meanwhile, toss liver in flour; shake off excess. Cook liver on heated oiled flat plate, uncovered, until cooked as desired.

4 Serve meat with vegetables, sprinkled with vinegar then oregano.

serves 4
per serving 39.6g fat; 2745kJ (656 cal)

tamarind-glazed riblets with rice noodle stir-fry

PREPARATION TIME 15 MINUTES (PLUS REFRIGERATION TIME) **COOKING TIME** 15 MINUTES

2 cloves garlic, crushed

2cm piece fresh ginger
(10g), grated

⅓ cup (80ml) chinese rice wine

¼ cup (55g) firmly packed
brown sugar

2 tablespoons kecap manis

1 tablespoon tamarind
concentrate

1 teaspoon sichuan
peppercorns, crushed

1kg lamb riblets

1 large carrot (180g)

2 large zucchini (300g)

500g fresh rice noodles

1 teaspoon sesame oil

6 green onions, cut into
8cm lengths

1 Combine garlic, ginger, wine, sugar, kecap manis, tamarind and
pepper in large bowl, add lamb; toss lamb to coat in marinade.
Cover; refrigerate overnight.

2 Drain lamb; reserve marinade. Cook lamb on heated oiled grill plate,
covered, over low heat about 15 minutes or until cooked as desired.

3 Meanwhile, using vegetable peeler, slice carrot and zucchini into ribbons.
Place noodles in large heatproof bowl, cover with boiling water, separate
with fork; drain.

4 Heat oil in wok; stir-fry carrot, zucchini and onion 1 minute. Add
reserved marinade; bring to a boil. Add noodles; stir-fry until heated
through. Serve lamb with stir-fry.

serves 4
per serving 17g fat; 1870kJ (447 cal)

lamb wrapped in prosciutto with herb risotto

PREPARATION TIME 10 MINUTES **COOKING TIME** 35 MINUTES

4 lamb backstraps (800g)
1 tablespoon sun-dried tomato pesto
8 slices prosciutto (120g)
1 litre (4 cups) chicken stock
½ cup (125ml) dry white wine
1 tablespoon olive oil
1 medium brown onion (150g), chopped finely
1 clove garlic, crushed
1½ cups (300g) arborio rice
⅓ cup (25g) finely grated parmesan cheese
⅓ cup loosely packed fresh chervil leaves
2 tablespoons fresh tarragon leaves
2 tablespoons finely chopped fresh chives
300g mushrooms, sliced thickly

1 Rub one side of each backstrap with one teaspoon of the pesto. Wrap each backstrap with two slices of prosciutto.
2 Combine stock and wine in medium saucepan; bring to a boil. Reduce heat; simmer, covered.
3 Heat oil in large saucepan; cook onion and garlic, stirring, until onion softens. Add rice; stir rice to coat in oil mixture. Stir in 1 cup simmering stock mixture; cook, stirring, over low heat until liquid is absorbed. Continue adding stock mixture, in 1-cup batches, stirring, until liquid is absorbed after each addition. Total cooking time should be about 35 minutes or until rice is just tender. Stir in cheese and herbs.
4 Meanwhile, cook lamb on heated oiled grill plate, uncovered, until cooked as desired. Cover lamb; stand 5 minutes, slice thickly.
5 Cook mushrooms on heated oiled flat plate, uncovered, until tender.
6 Serve lamb with risotto and mushrooms.

serves 4
per serving 27.7g fat; 3242kJ (775 cal)

pork chops with cranberry sauce and kumara craisin salad

PREPARATION TIME 15 MINUTES **COOKING TIME** 30 MINUTES

1 tablespoon ground ginger

1 tablespoon ground coriander

1 teaspoon sweet paprika

½ cup (160g) cranberry sauce

2 tablespoons orange juice

2 tablespoons lemon juice

1 tablespoon dijon mustard

4 pork loin chops (1.2kg)

KUMARA CRAISIN SALAD

3 large kumara (1.5kg), diced into 2cm pieces

2 tablespoons olive oil

½ cup (80g) toasted pine nuts

⅓ cup (50g) craisins

1 cup coarsely chopped fresh coriander

¼ cup (60ml) white wine vinegar

2 teaspoons olive oil, extra

1 Combine ginger, coriander, paprika, sauce, juices and mustard in large bowl, add pork; toss pork to coat in mixture.

2 Make kumara craisin salad.

3 Cook pork on heated oiled grill plate, uncovered, until cooked as desired. Serve pork with salad.

KUMARA CRAISIN SALAD Boil, steam or microwave kumara until just tender; drain. Combine kumara with oil in large bowl; cook kumara on heated oiled flat plate, uncovered, until browned lightly. Return kumara to same bowl with remaining ingredients; toss gently to combine.

serves 4

per serving 45.6g fat; 3625kJ (866 cal)

pork burgers with caramelised pears

PREPARATION TIME 15 MINUTES **COOKING TIME** 15 MINUTES

We used corella pears – small pears with pale flesh and a mild flavour – for this recipe.
Dijonnaise is a commercial blend of mayonnaise and dijon mustard, available in most supermarkets.

500g pork mince
2 cloves garlic, crushed
3 green onions, chopped finely
1 fresh small red thai chilli,
  chopped finely
1 egg
2 tablespoons barbecue sauce
½ cup (35g) stale breadcrumbs
4 small pears (720g), sliced thinly
1 medium red onion (170g),
  sliced thinly
¼ cup (60ml) balsamic vinegar
1 tablespoon brown sugar
1 long french bread stick (350g)
2 tablespoons dijonnaise
50g mizuna

1 Using hand, combine mince,
   garlic, green onion, chilli, egg,
   sauce and breadcrumbs in
   medium bowl; shape mixture
   into four burgers. Cook burgers
   on heated oiled flat plate,
   uncovered, until cooked through.
2 Meanwhile, cook pear and red
   onion on heated oiled flat plate,
   uncovered, until onion softens.
   Sprinkle combined vinegar and
   sugar over pear and red onion;
   cook, turning, about 10 minutes
   or until mixture caramelises.
3 Cut bread into quarters; split
   quarters in half horizontally.
   Spread dijonnaise on cut sides;
   sandwich mizuna, burgers and
   caramelised pear and red onion
   between bread pieces.

serves 4
per serving 16.9g fat;
2644kJ (632 cal)

five-spice pork belly ribs with crunchy noodle salad

PREPARATION TIME 20 MINUTES (PLUS REFRIGERATION TIME) **COOKING TIME** 20 MINUTES

3 cloves garlic, crushed

3cm piece fresh ginger (15g), grated

1½ teaspoons five-spice powder

¼ cup (85g) orange marmalade

¼ cup (90g) honey

2 tablespoons kecap manis

1.5kg pork belly ribs

CRUNCHY NOODLE SALAD

10 trimmed red radishes (150g),
  sliced thinly

1 large red capsicum (350g),
  sliced thinly

½ small chinese cabbage (350g),
  shredded finely

6 green onions, chopped finely

100g packet fried noodles

¼ cup (60ml) white vinegar

¼ cup (55g) firmly packed
  brown sugar

¼ cup (60ml) soy sauce

2 teaspoons sesame oil

1 clove garlic, crushed

1 Combine garlic, ginger, five-spice, marmalade, honey and kecap manis in large bowl, add pork; toss pork to coat in marinade. Cover; refrigerate overnight.

2 Drain pork; reserve marinade. Cook pork on heated oiled grill plate, uncovered, brushing occasionally with reserved marinade, until cooked through.

3 Meanwhile, make crunchy noodle salad. Serve pork with salad.

CRUNCHY NOODLE SALAD
Combine radish, capsicum, cabbage, onion and noodles in large bowl. Place remaining ingredients in screw-top jar; shake well. Pour dressing over salad; toss gently to combine.

serves 4
per serving 24.8g fat;
2763kJ (660 cal)

pork medallions with gnocchi salad

PREPARATION TIME 15 MINUTES **COOKING TIME** 25 MINUTES

1 tablespoon olive oil

1 tablespoon balsamic vinegar

1 clove garlic, crushed

800g pork fillets

1 medium red onion (170g), cut into wedges

1 medium red capsicum (200g), quartered

1 medium yellow capsicum (200g), quartered

500g packet potato gnocchi

250g grape tomatoes, halved

1 cup loosely packed fresh basil leaves, torn

1 cup (150g) seeded kalamata olives

BALSAMIC DRESSING

2 tablespoons olive oil

2 tablespoons balsamic vinegar

1 clove garlic, crushed

1 teaspoon dijon mustard

1 Combine oil, vinegar and garlic in large bowl, add pork; toss pork to coat in mixture. Make balsamic dressing.

2 Cook onion and capsicums on heated oiled grill plate, uncovered, until tender; slice capsicums thickly. Place onion and capsicums in large bowl; cover to keep warm.

3 Meanwhile, cook gnocchi in large saucepan of boiling water, uncovered, until gnocchi float to the surface. Remove from pan with slotted spoon; place in bowl with grilled vegetables.

4 Cook pork on heated oiled grill plate, uncovered, until cooked as desired. Cover pork; stand 5 minutes, slice thickly.

5 Add dressing, tomato, basil and olives to bowl with grilled vegetables and gnocchi; toss gently to combine. Serve pork with salad.

BALSAMIC DRESSING Place ingredients in screw-top jar; shake well.

serves 4
per serving 20g fat; 2101kJ (502 cal)

sichuan pepper pork with peach and chilli salad

PREPARATION TIME 15 MINUTES **COOKING TIME** 20 MINUTES

¼ cup (35g) sichuan
  peppercorns
¼ cup coriander seeds
2 tablespoons brown sugar
¼ cup (60ml) olive oil
700g pork fillets, halved
  lengthways

PEACH AND CHILLI SALAD
2 large peaches (440g), quartered
1 fresh long red chilli,
  seeded, sliced thinly
¼ cup loosely packed
  fresh coriander leaves
¼ cup loosely packed
  fresh mint leaves
100g baby spinach leaves
2 tablespoons lemon juice
1 tablespoon olive oil

1 Dry-fry peppercorns and seeds
  over medium heat in small
  frying pan until fragrant. Using
  mortar and pestle, crush spices
  with sugar and oil; press spice
  mixture all over pork.
2 Cook pork on heated oiled flat
  plate, uncovered, until cooked
  as desired. Cover pork; stand
  5 minutes, slice thinly.
3 Meanwhile, make peach and
  chilli salad; serve with pork.

PEACH AND CHILLI SALAD
Cook peach on heated oiled flat
plate, uncovered, until softened.
Place peach in large bowl with
remaining ingredients; toss gently
to combine.

serves 4
per serving 22.5g fat;
1730kJ (413 cal)

tex-mex spareribs with grilled corn salsa

PREPARATION TIME 15 MINUTES **COOKING TIME** 25 MINUTES

2 tablespoons brown sugar

1 tablespoon dried oregano

2 tablespoons sweet paprika

2 teaspoons cracked
black pepper

½ teaspoon cayenne pepper

1 tablespoon ground cumin

1 tablespoon garlic powder

¼ cup (60ml) water

2 tablespoons vegetable oil

1.5kg American-style
pork spareribs

3 trimmed corn cobs (750g)

2 medium tomatoes (300g),
seeded, chopped finely

1 long green chilli,
chopped finely

1 medium red onion (170g),
chopped finely

1 medium green capsicum (200g),
chopped finely

¼ cup coarsely chopped
fresh coriander

2 tablespoons lime juice

1 tablespoon olive oil

1 Combine sugar, oregano, spices, the water and oil in large bowl; add pork, rub spice mixture all over pork. Cook pork on heated oiled flat plate, uncovered, until cooked as desired.

2 Meanwhile, cook corn on heated oiled grill plate, uncovered, until tender. When cool enough to handle, cut kernels from cobs. Place kernels in medium bowl with remaining ingredients; toss salsa gently to combine. Serve with pork.

serves 4
per serving 28.2g fat;
2594kJ (620 cal)

margarita-marinated loin chops with orange and watercress salad

PREPARATION TIME 15 MINUTES (PLUS REFRIGERATION TIME) **COOKING TIME** 15 MINUTES

¼ cup (60ml) lime juice

2 fresh small red thai chillies, seeded, chopped finely

2 cloves garlic, crushed

½ cup (170g) orange marmalade

⅓ cup finely chopped fresh coriander

½ cup (125ml) tequila

8 pork loin chops (2.2kg)

ORANGE AND WATERCRESS SALAD

2 large oranges (600g)

¼ cup (60ml) lime juice

¼ cup (85g) orange marmalade

2 tablespoons olive oil

2 teaspoons tequila

100g watercress, trimmed

1 medium avocado (250g), sliced thinly

½ cup loosely packed fresh coriander leaves

1 Combine juice, chilli, garlic, marmalade, coriander and tequila, add pork; toss pork to coat in marinade. Cover; refrigerate overnight.

2 Make orange and watercress salad.

3 Drain pork; reserve marinade. Cook pork on heated oiled grill plate, uncovered, brushing occasionally with marinade, until cooked as desired. Serve pork with salad.

ORANGE AND WATERCRESS SALAD Segment oranges over large bowl; stir in juice, marmalade and oil. Add remaining ingredients; toss gently to combine.

serves 4

per serving 58.6g fat; 4762kJ (1138 cal)

pork schnitzel with pesto butter

PREPARATION TIME 25 MINUTES **COOKING TIME** 10 MINUTES

⅓ cup (80ml) lemon juice

2 tablespoons olive oil

3 cloves garlic, crushed

1 tablespoon fresh
  thyme leaves

8 pork schnitzels (800g)

500g kipfler potatoes, halved

PESTO BUTTER

60g butter, softened

⅓ cup coarsely chopped
  fresh basil

¼ cup (40g) toasted pine nuts

1 clove garlic, quartered

2 tablespoons coarsely grated
  parmesan cheese

1 Combine juice, oil, garlic and
   thyme in medium bowl, add
   pork; toss pork to coat in mixture.

2 Meanwhile, boil, steam or
   microwave potato until tender;
   drain. Make pesto butter. Toss
   half of the pesto butter with
   potato in medium bowl; cover
   to keep warm.

3 Cook pork on heated oiled grill
   plate, uncovered, until cooked
   as desired. Drizzle pork with
   remaining pesto butter; serve
   with potato.

PESTO BUTTER Blend or
process ingredients until smooth.

serves 4
per serving 32.4g fat; 2388kJ
(571 cal)

italian BLT

PREPARATION TIME 15 MINUTES **COOKING TIME** 15 MINUTES

4 medium egg tomatoes (300g),
    quartered
1 tablespoon balsamic vinegar
1 tablespoon finely chopped
    fresh basil
¼ cup (60ml) olive oil
8 slices pancetta (120g)
1 loaf ciabatta (350g)
1 clove garlic, crushed
100g bocconcini, sliced thickly
25g baby rocket leaves

1 Place tomato in medium
   bowl with vinegar, basil and
   1 tablespoon of the oil; toss
   tomato to coat in mixture.
2 Cook tomato and pancetta
   on heated oiled flat plate,
   uncovered, until tomato is
   browned and pancetta crisp.
3 Cut bread into quarters, split
   quarters in half horizontally;
   brush cut sides with combined
   garlic and remaining oil. Toast
   bread, cut-side down, on heated
   flat plate.
4 Sandwich tomato, pancetta,
   bocconcini and rocket between
   bread pieces.

serves 4
per serving 24g fat;
1903kJ (455 cal)

paprika and cumin-spiced cutlets with carrot and olive salad

PREPARATION TIME 20 MINUTES **COOKING TIME** 20 MINUTES

2 tablespoons olive oil
¼ cup (60ml) lemon juice
2 teaspoons ground cumin
1 tablespoon sweet paprika
4 pork cutlets (1kg)

CARROT AND OLIVE SALAD
4 medium carrots (480g), halved lengthways, sliced thinly
1 cup (120g) seeded black olives, chopped coarsely
½ cup loosely packed fresh flat-leaf parsley leaves
½ cup loosely packed fresh coriander leaves
2 tablespoons olive oil
2 teaspoons ground cumin
1 tablespoon red wine vinegar
2 teaspoons harissa

1 Combine oil, juice, cumin and paprika in large bowl, add pork; toss pork to coat in mixture.
2 Cook pork on heated oiled grill plate, uncovered, until cooked as desired.
3 Meanwhile, make carrot and olive salad.
4 Serve pork with salad.

CARROT AND OLIVE SALAD Boil, steam or microwave carrot until just tender; drain. Cool 10 minutes. Place carrot in medium bowl with olives, herbs and combined remaining ingredients; toss gently to combine.

serves 4
per serving 35.8g fat; 2033kJ (485 cal)

pork satay with grilled baby bok choy

PREPARATION TIME 10 MINUTES **COOKING TIME** 25 MINUTES

1 tablespoon peanut oil
1 small brown onion (80g),
   chopped finely
2 cloves garlic, crushed
2 fresh small red thai chillies,
   seeded, chopped finely
½ cup (140g) peanut butter
1 tablespoon fish sauce
1 tablespoon kecap manis
140ml can coconut cream
½ cup (125ml) orange juice
½ cup (75g) coarsely chopped
   unsalted toasted peanuts
800g pork fillets
800g baby bok choy,
   halved lengthways

1 Heat half of the oil in medium
   saucepan; cook onion, garlic
   and chilli, stirring, until onion
   softens. Add peanut butter,
   sauces, coconut cream, juice
   and nuts; bring to a boil. Reduce
   heat; simmer, uncovered, about
   5 minutes or until mixture thickens
   slightly. Cover to keep warm.
2 Cook pork on heated oiled grill
   plate, uncovered, until cooked
   as desired. Cover pork; stand
   5 minutes, slice thickly.
3 Meanwhile, boil, steam or
   microwave bok choy until
   leaves just wilt; drain. Brush
   bok choy with remaining oil;
   cook on heated oiled grill plate,
   uncovered, until tender.
4 Serve pork and bok choy with
   satay sauce and steamed
   jasmine rice, if desired.

serves 4
per serving 43.4g fat;
2867kJ (685 cal)

sausages with warm pear and witlof salad

PREPARATION TIME 15 MINUTES **COOKING TIME** 15 MINUTES

2 medium red onions (340g),
    cut into wedges
1 tablespoon caraway seeds
3 medium pears (690g), cut
    into wedges
¼ cup (60ml) apple cider vinegar
2 tablespoons olive oil
8 thick pork sausages (960g)
1 cup (140g) toasted pecans
2 witlof (250g), trimmed,
    separated into leaves,
    halved lengthways

1 Cook onion on heated oiled
   flat plate until softened. Add
   caraway seeds and pear; cook,
   uncovered, about 5 minutes
   or until pear is browned lightly.
   Place pear mixture in medium
   bowl with vinegar and oil.

2 Meanwhile, cook sausages
   on heated oiled grill plate,
   uncovered, until cooked through.

3 Place nuts and witlof in bowl
   with pear mixture; toss gently
   to combine. Serve salad
   with sausages.

serves 4
per serving 88g fat;
4421kJ (1056 cal)

asian chicken burger with pickled cucumber and wasabi mayonnaise

PREPARATION TIME 15 MINUTES (PLUS REFRIGERATION TIME) **COOKING TIME** 15 MINUTES

500g chicken mince
1 tablespoon soy sauce
1 egg
1 cup (70g) stale breadcrumbs
1 teaspoon sesame oil
2 green onions, chopped finely
4 hamburger buns
50g mizuna

PICKLED CUCUMBER
1 lebanese cucumber (130g)
¼ cup (70g) drained pickled pink ginger
½ cup (125ml) rice vinegar
1 teaspoon salt
1 tablespoon sugar

WASABI MAYONNAISE
¼ cup (75g) mayonnaise
2 teaspoons wasabi paste

1 Make pickled cucumber. Make wasabi mayonnaise.
2 Meanwhile, using hand, combine mince, sauce, egg, breadcrumbs, oil and onion in large bowl; shape mixture into four burgers.
3 Cook burgers on heated oiled flat plate, uncovered, about 15 minutes or until cooked through.
4 Meanwhile, split buns in half horizontally; toast, cut-side up. Spread wasabi mayonnaise on bun bases; sandwich mizuna, burgers and drained pickled cucumber between bun halves.

PICKLED CUCUMBER Using sharp knife, mandoline or v-slicer, slice cucumber thinly. Combine cucumber in small bowl with remaining ingredients. Cover; refrigerate 30 minutes.
WASABI MAYONNAISE Combine ingredients in small bowl.

serves 4
per serving 21.7g fat; 2238kJ (535 cal)

cajun chicken with pineapple salsa

PREPARATION TIME 15 MINUTES **COOKING TIME** 15 MINUTES

1 tablespoon sweet paprika
1 teaspoon cayenne pepper
2 teaspoons garlic powder
2 teaspoons dried oregano
1 tablespoon olive oil
8 chicken thigh fillets (880g)

PINEAPPLE SALSA
4 bacon rashers (280g),
   rind removed
1 small pineapple (800g),
   chopped finely
1 fresh small red thai chilli,
   chopped finely
¼ cup coarsely chopped fresh
   flat-leaf parsley
1 medium red capsicum (200g),
   chopped coarsely
¼ cup (60ml) lime juice
1 teaspoon olive oil

1 Combine spices, oregano and
   oil in large bowl, add chicken;
   toss chicken to coat in mixture.
2 Make pineapple salsa.
3 Meanwhile, cook chicken on
   heated oiled flat plate, uncovered,
   until cooked through.
4 Serve chicken with salsa and
   lemon wedges, if desired.

PINEAPPLE SALSA Cook
bacon on heated oiled flat
plate, uncovered, until crisp;
drain then chop coarsely. Place
bacon in medium bowl with
remaining ingredients; toss
gently to combine.

serves 4
per serving 24.1g fat;
1991kJ (476 cal)

balsamic chicken with rosemary potatoes

PREPARATION TIME 10 MINUTES **COOKING TIME** 20 MINUTES

¼ cup (60ml) balsamic vinegar
¼ cup (60ml) olive oil
2 tablespoons fresh
   rosemary leaves
6 chicken thigh fillets (660g)
700g potatoes, diced into
   2cm pieces
6 medium zucchini (720g),
   sliced thickly

1 Combine vinegar, 2 tablespoons
of the oil and half of the rosemary
in medium bowl, add chicken;
toss chicken to coat in marinade.

2 Boil, steam or microwave potato
until just tender; drain.

3 Drain chicken; reserve marinade.
Cook chicken on heated oiled
grill plate, uncovered, until
cooked through.

4 Meanwhile, toss potato in
medium bowl with remaining
rosemary and remaining oil. Cook
potato, on heated oiled flat plate,
uncovered, until tender.

5 Cook zucchini on flat plate,
uncovered, brushing with
reserved marinade, until
browned lightly.

6 Slice chicken pieces in half;
serve with potato and zucchini.

serves 4
per serving 26.1g fat;
1967kJ (470 cal)

chicken wings and green mango salad

PREPARATION TIME 20 MINUTES (PLUS REFRIGERATION TIME) **COOKING TIME** 15 MINUTES

10cm stick (20g) fresh lemon grass, chopped finely
1 long green chilli, chopped finely
3 cloves garlic, crushed
10 fresh kaffir lime leaves, shredded finely
16 chicken wings (1.5kg)
2 small green mangoes (600g)
1 large carrot (180g)
1 lebanese cucumber (130g)
1 medium red capsicum (200g), sliced thinly
2 green onions, sliced thinly

SWEET AND SOUR DRESSING
2 tablespoons fish sauce
2 tablespoons lime juice
2 tablespoons grated palm sugar
1 tablespoon white vinegar
1 tablespoon water

1 Make sweet and sour dressing.
2 Combine lemon grass, chilli, garlic, about half of the lime leaves and 2 tablespoons of the dressing in medium bowl, add chicken; toss chicken to coat in marinade. Cover remaining dressing and chicken separately; refrigerate overnight.
3 Drain chicken; discard marinade. Cook chicken on heated oiled grill plate, uncovered, until cooked through.
4 Meanwhile, use vegetable peeler to finely slice mangoes, carrot and cucumber into ribbons. Place in medium bowl with capsicum, remaining lime leaves and remaining dressing; toss gently to combine. Serve chicken with salad, sprinkled with onion.

SWEET AND SOUR DRESSING Place ingredients in screw-top jar; shake well.

serves 4
per serving 13g fat; 1883kJ (450 cal)

harissa chicken with couscous salad

PREPARATION TIME 15 MINUTES **COOKING TIME** 15 MINUTES

Harissa, a North African paste made from dried red chillies, garlic, olive oil and caraway seeds, can be used as a rub for meat, an ingredient in sauces and dressings, or eaten on its own, as a condiment. It is available ready-made from Middle-Eastern food shops and some supermarkets.

2 tablespoons harissa
2 teaspoons finely grated
   lemon rind
800g chicken breast fillets,
   sliced thickly

COUSCOUS SALAD
1½ cups (375ml) chicken stock
2 teaspoons ground coriander
1½ cups (300g) couscous
1 medium red capsicum (200g),
   chopped finely
1 medium brown onion (150g),
   chopped finely
3 green onions, sliced thinly
½ cup firmly packed fresh
   coriander leaves
⅓ cup (80ml) lemon juice
1 tablespoon olive oil

1 Combine harissa and rind in
   medium bowl, add chicken;
   toss chicken to coat in mixture.
2 Make couscous salad.
3 Meanwhile, cook chicken on heated
   oiled grill plate, uncovered, until
   cooked through. Cover chicken;
   stand 5 minutes, slice thickly.
4 Serve chicken on salad.

COUSCOUS SALAD Bring stock
and ground coriander to a boil in
medium saucepan. Remove from
heat; stir in couscous. Cover; stand
about 5 minutes or until liquid is
absorbed, fluffing occasionally with
fork. Add remaining ingredients; toss
gently to combine.

serves 4
per serving 10.3g fat;
2454kJ (586 cal)

citrus chicken with char-grilled orange and corn

PREPARATION TIME 10 MINUTES (PLUS REFRIGERATION TIME) **COOKING TIME** 20 MINUTES

⅔ cup (160ml) lemon juice

¾ cup (180ml) orange juice

3 cloves garlic, crushed

1 tablespoon finely chopped
fresh oregano

1 teaspoon ground cumin

1 fresh small red thai chilli,
chopped finely

1 tablespoon olive oil

4 single chicken breast
fillets (680g)

3 trimmed corn cobs (750g),
quartered

1 large orange (300g), unpeeled,
cut into 8 wedges

8 green onions, cut into
8cm lengths

1 Combine juices, garlic, oregano, cumin, chilli and oil in medium bowl, add chicken; toss chicken to coat in marinade. Cover; refrigerate overnight.

2 Drain chicken; reserve marinade. Cook chicken on heated oiled grill plate, uncovered, until cooked through.

3 Meanwhile, cook corn, orange and onion on heated oiled grill plate, uncovered, until tender.

4 Place reserved marinade in small saucepan; bring to a boil. Reduce heat; simmer, uncovered, 2 minutes. Serve chicken with corn, orange and onion, drizzled with marinade.

serves 4
per serving 10.4g fat;
1732kJ (414 cal)

chicken kofta with red capsicum and walnut sauce

PREPARATION TIME 20 MINUTES (PLUS REFRIGERATION TIME) **COOKING TIME** 20 MINUTES

You need 12 bamboo skewers for this recipe. Soak them in cold water before use to prevent them from splintering and scorching.

700g chicken mince

1 large brown onion (200g), chopped finely

1½ cups (110g) stale breadcrumbs

1 egg

¼ cup finely chopped fresh coriander

½ teaspoon ground cinnamon

3 teaspoons ground cumin

2 teaspoons ground allspice

6 pitta pockets, halved

100g baby rocket leaves

RED CAPSICUM AND
WALNUT SAUCE

2 medium red capsicums (400g)

⅓ cup (35g) toasted walnuts

2 tablespoons stale breadcrumbs

2 tablespoons lemon juice

1 teaspoon sambal oelek

½ teaspoon ground cumin

2 tablespoons olive oil

1 Using hand, combine mince, onion, breadcrumbs, egg, coriander and spices in large bowl; shape ¼-cups of the mixture around each skewer to form slightly flattened sausage shapes. Place kofta on tray, cover; refrigerate 10 minutes.

2 Meanwhile, make red capsicum and walnut sauce.

3 Cook kofta on heated oiled grill plate, uncovered, about 15 minutes or until cooked through. Serve kofta with warm pitta, rocket and sauce.

RED CAPSICUM AND WALNUT SAUCE Quarter capsicums; discard seeds and membranes. Cook on heated oiled grill plate, skin-side down, uncovered, until skin blisters and blackens. Cover capsicum pieces with plastic wrap or paper for 5 minutes; peel away skin. Blend or process capsicum with remaining ingredients until smooth.

serves 4
per serving 34.5g fat; 3710kJ (886 cal)

chilli lime chicken on lemon grass skewers with thai noodle salad

PREPARATION TIME 20 MINUTES (PLUS REFRIGERATION TIME) **COOKING TIME** 20 MINUTES

1kg chicken breast fillets,
  diced into 3cm pieces
6 x 15cm-long fresh lemon grass sticks,
  halved lengthways
2 tablespoons peanut oil
1 tablespoon finely grated lime rind
2 tablespoons finely chopped
  fresh coriander
1 fresh small red thai chilli, chopped finely

THAI NOODLE SALAD
200g bean thread noodles
10cm stick (20g) fresh lemon grass,
  chopped finely
2 tablespoons lime juice
1 clove garlic, crushed
1 fresh small red thai chilli, chopped finely
2 tablespoons fish sauce
1 tablespoon water
1 tablespoon rice vinegar
4 green onions, chopped coarsely
1 medium red capsicum (200g), sliced thinly

1 Using tip of small knife, cut slit through centre of each piece of chicken; thread chicken onto lemon grass skewers. Combine oil, rind, coriander and chilli in shallow baking dish, add skewers; turn skewers to coat in marinade. Cover; refrigerate overnight.
2 Make thai noodle salad.
3 Meanwhile, drain skewers; discard marinade. Cook skewers on heated oiled grill plate, uncovered, until cooked through. Serve chicken skewers with salad.

THAI NOODLE SALAD Place noodles in large heatproof bowl, cover with boiling water; stand until just tender, drain. When cool enough to handle, using kitchen scissors, cut noodles into random lengths; cool 10 minutes. Combine lemon grass, juice, garlic, chilli, sauce, the water and vinegar in large bowl; add noodles with onion and capsicum, toss gently to combine.

serves 4
per serving 15.4g fat; 2000kJ (478 cal)

quail, fig and orange salad

PREPARATION TIME 15 MINUTES **COOKING TIME** 20 MINUTES

6 quails (1.2kg)

3 medium oranges (720g)

4 medium fresh figs (240g),
    quartered

100g mizuna

½ cup (60g) coarsely chopped
    toasted pecans

MAPLE ORANGE DRESSING

⅓ cup (80ml) orange juice

¼ cup (60ml) olive oil

2 tablespoons pure
    maple syrup

1 clove garlic, crushed

1 Make maple orange dressing.

2 Rinse quails under cold water; pat dry with absorbent paper. Discard necks from quails. Using kitchen scissors, cut along each side of each quail's backbone; discard backbones. Halve each quail along breastbone; brush quail halves with half of the dressing. Cook quail on heated oiled grill plate, uncovered, until cooked through.

3 Meanwhile, segment oranges over large bowl; add remaining ingredients and remaining dressing, toss gently to combine.

4 Divide salad among serving plates; top with quails.

MAPLE ORANGE DRESSING Place ingredients in screw-top jar; shake well.

serves 4
per serving 43.6g fat; 2644kJ (632 cal)

nam jim with butterflied spatchcock

PREPARATION TIME 15 MINUTES **COOKING TIME** 25 MINUTES

Nam jim is a generic term for a Thai dipping sauce; most versions include fish sauce and chillies, but the remaining ingredients are up to the individual cook's discretion.

4 spatchcocks (2kg)
⅓ cup (90g) grated palm sugar
2 teaspoons ground cumin
1 teaspoon salt
2 lebanese cucumbers (260g), seeded, sliced thinly
½ cup firmly packed fresh mint leaves
1 cup firmly packed fresh thai basil leaves
1 cup firmly packed fresh coriander leaves

NAM JIM
2 cloves garlic, chopped coarsely
3 long green chillies, seeded, chopped coarsely
2 teaspoons finely chopped coriander root
1 tablespoon fish sauce
1 tablespoon grated palm sugar
2 shallots (50g), chopped coarsely
¼ cup (60ml) lime juice

1 Rinse spatchcocks under cold water; pat dry with absorbent paper. Using kitchen scissors, cut along each side of each spatchcock's backbone; discard backbones. Turn each spatchcock skin-side up; use heel of hand to press flat. Using fork, prick skin several times. Rub each spatchcock with combined sugar, cumin and salt; stand 5 minutes.

2 Meanwhile, make nam jim.

3 Cook spatchcocks on heated oiled grill plate, covered, over low heat about 20 minutes or until cooked through.

4 Meanwhile, place remaining ingredients in large bowl with 2 tablespoons of the nam jim; toss gently to combine.

5 Serve spatchcocks with salad and remaining nam jim.

NAM JIM Blend or process ingredients until smooth.

serves 4
per serving 23.4g fat; 2731kJ (652 cal)

grilled chicken wings with ranch dressing and rocket and blue cheese salad

PREPARATION TIME 10 MINUTES **COOKING TIME** 20 MINUTES

Buy the best quality whole egg mayonnaise you can find for this recipe (if you don't make your own) because the sweetness of some commercial mayonnaise will spoil the taste of the ranch dressing.

12 chicken wings (1kg)
1 tablespoon olive oil

RANCH DRESSING
⅓ cup (95g) yogurt
⅓ cup (100g) mayonnaise
2 tablespoons buttermilk
1 small brown onion (80g), grated finely
1 clove garlic, crushed
1 tablespoon finely chopped fresh chives

ROCKET AND BLUE CHEESE SALAD
100g baby rocket leaves
250g grape tomatoes, halved
1 tablespoon olive oil
2 tablespoons red wine vinegar
100g blue cheese, cut into 4 wedges

1 Cut wing tips from chicken; discard tips. Cut wings in half at joints. Brush wings with oil; cook on heated oiled grill plate, uncovered, until cooked through.
2 Meanwhile, make ranch dressing and rocket and blue cheese salad.
3 Serve chicken with salad and ranch dressing.

RANCH DRESSING Combine ingredients in small bowl.
ROCKET AND BLUE CHEESE SALAD Combine rocket, tomato, oil and vinegar in medium bowl; top with cheese.

serves 4
per serving 34.9g fat;
2220kJ (530 cal)

stuffed chicken breast with spinach salad

PREPARATION TIME 10 MINUTES **COOKING TIME** 20 MINUTES

4 single chicken breast
  fillets (680g)
80g fontina cheese, sliced thinly
4 slices bottled char-grilled
  red capsicum (170g)
100g baby spinach leaves
1 medium lemon (140g)
2 medium oranges (480g)
1 small red onion (100g),
  sliced thinly
1 tablespoon olive oil

1 Using tip of small knife, slit a pocket in one side of each fillet, taking care not to cut all the way through. Divide cheese, capsicum and a few spinach leaves among pockets; secure with toothpicks.

2 Cook chicken on heated oiled grill plate, uncovered, until cooked through. Cover chicken; stand 10 minutes. Remove toothpicks; slice thickly.

3 Meanwhile, segment lemon and orange over large bowl, add onion, oil and remaining spinach; toss gently to combine.

4 Serve chicken with salad.

serves 4
per serving 18g fat;
1930kJ (461 cal)

grilled turkey steaks with green olive and tomato relish

PREPARATION TIME 10 MINUTES **COOKING TIME** 30 MINUTES

1kg potatoes

4 turkey steaks (800g)

1 teaspoon sea salt

½ teaspoon cracked
    black pepper

GREEN OLIVE AND
TOMATO RELISH

1 tablespoon extra virgin
    olive oil

1 small red onion (100g),
    chopped finely

1 clove garlic, crushed

2 large green tomatoes (440g),
    chopped finely

2 cups (240g) seeded green
    olives, chopped finely

2 tablespoons sugar

¼ cup (60ml) apple cider vinegar

2 tablespoons drained capers,
    rinsed, chopped finely

⅓ cup finely chopped fresh
    flat-leaf parsley

1 Make green olive and tomato relish.

2 Meanwhile, cut potatoes into 1cm slices; cook on heated oiled grill plate, uncovered, until tender.

3 Sprinkle turkey with salt and pepper; cook on heated oiled grill plate, uncovered, until cooked through. Serve turkey with potato and relish.

GREEN OLIVE AND TOMATO RELISH Heat oil in medium saucepan; cook onion and garlic, stirring, until onion softens. Add tomato, olives, sugar and vinegar; cook, stirring occasionally, 10 minutes. Remove from heat; stir in capers and parsley.

serves 4
per serving 12.1g fat; 2254kJ (538 cal)

TIP The relish can be stored, covered, in the refrigerator for up to two weeks.

seafood

thai fish burgers
with sour and sweet green salad

PREPARATION TIME 20 MINUTES **COOKING TIME** 15 MINUTES

You need to buy a very small iceberg lettuce for this recipe. We used blue-eye fillets here, but you can substitute them with any firm white fish fillets you like.

500g blue-eye fillets, chopped coarsely
1 tablespoon fish sauce
1 tablespoon kecap manis
1 clove garlic, quartered
1 fresh small red thai chilli, quartered
50g green beans, trimmed, chopped coarsely
¼ cup (15g) shredded coconut
¼ cup finely chopped fresh coriander
½ loaf turkish bread (215g)
⅓ cup (80ml) sweet chilli sauce

SOUR AND SWEET GREEN SALAD
2 cups (120g) finely shredded iceberg lettuce
40g snow pea sprouts, chopped coarsely
1 telegraph cucumber (400g), seeded, sliced thinly
2 tablespoons lime juice
1 tablespoon fish sauce
1 tablespoon brown sugar

1 Blend or process fillets, sauce, kecap manis, garlic and chilli until smooth. Place in large bowl with beans, coconut and coriander; using hand, combine ingredients then shape mixture into four burgers.
2 Cook burgers on heated oiled flat plate, covered, about 15 minutes or until cooked through.
3 Meanwhile, make sour and sweet green salad.
4 Cut bread in half; split halves horizontally. Toast, cut-side up. Divide bread among serving plates; top with salad, burgers and chilli sauce.

SOUR AND SWEET GREEN SALAD Place ingredients in medium bowl; toss gently to combine.

serves 4
per serving 8.1g fat; 1491kJ (356 cal)

salmon steaks with tarragon sauce and grilled asparagus

PREPARATION TIME 10 MINUTES **COOKING TIME** 25 MINUTES

800g potatoes, sliced thickly
500g asparagus, trimmed
4 salmon fillets (800g)

TARRAGON SAUCE
20g butter
1 medium brown onion (150g),
   chopped finely
½ cup (125ml) dry white wine
300ml cream
2 tablespoons finely chopped
   fresh tarragon

1 Make tarragon sauce.
2 Meanwhile, boil, steam or
   microwave potato until just
   tender; drain.
3 Cook potato, asparagus
   and fish on heated oiled grill
   plate, uncovered, until potato
   is browned, asparagus just
   tender and fish is cooked as
   desired. Serve fish with potato,
   asparagus and sauce.

TARRAGON SAUCE Melt
butter in small saucepan; cook
onion, stirring, until soft. Add
wine; bring to a boil. Reduce
heat; simmer, uncovered, until
liquid reduces by half. Add
cream; simmer, uncovered,
about 10 minutes or until sauce
thickens slightly. Remove from
heat; stir in tarragon.

serves 4
per serving 46g fat;
3166kJ (756 cal)

balmain bugs and citrus salad

PREPARATION TIME 20 MINUTES **COOKING TIME** 15 MINUTES

Large king prawns or scampi are good substitutes for the bugs in this recipe.

2kg uncooked balmain bugs
1 tablespoon olive oil
2 tablespoons orange juice
2 teaspoons finely grated
    orange rind
1 tablespoon wholegrain mustard

CITRUS SALAD
1 medium grapefruit (425g)
1 large orange (300g)
1 lemon (140g)
150g curly endive,
    chopped coarsely
1 large fennel bulb (550g),
    trimmed, sliced thinly
1 tablespoon wholegrain mustard
1 tablespoon olive oil

1 Make citrus salad.
2 Place balmain bugs upside
   down on chopping board; cut
   tail from body, discard body.
   Halve tail lengthways; discard
   back vein. Cook bugs on heated
   oiled grill plate, uncovered, until
   cooked through.
3 Place bugs in large bowl with
   combined oil, juice, rind and
   mustard; toss bugs to coat in
   mixture. Serve with citrus salad.

CITRUS SALAD Cut unpeeled
grapefruit, orange and lemon
into equal size wedges; cook on
heated oiled grill plate, uncovered,
until browned. Place fruit in large
bowl with endive, fennel and
combined mustard and oil; toss
gently to combine.

serves 4
per serving 12g fat;
1649kJ (394 cal)

79

calamari teppanyaki

PREPARATION TIME 20 MINUTES **COOKING TIME** 10 MINUTES

Teppanyaki is the name given to a traditional Japanese cooking style where the food is cooked rapidly on a searingly hot grill plate on or near the table. Pink pickled ginger, also known as gari, can be found in most Asian grocery stores.

1½ cups (300g) white medium-grain rice
3 cups (750ml) water
1 tablespoon peanut oil
1 fresh small red thai chilli, seeded, chopped finely
1 teaspoon finely grated lemon rind
1 clove garlic, crushed
1kg calamari rings
2 tablespoons drained pickled pink ginger, sliced thinly
6 green onions, sliced thickly
2 lebanese cucumbers (260g), seeded, chopped finely
3 fresh small red thai chillies, seeded, chopped finely, extra

LEMON SOY DIPPING SAUCE
¼ cup (60ml) rice vinegar
1 tablespoon sugar
1 tablespoon japanese soy sauce
1 teaspoon finely grated lemon rind

1 Make lemon soy dipping sauce.
2 Combine rice and the water in medium heavy-based saucepan, cover; bring to a boil, stirring occasionally. Reduce heat; simmer rice, covered tightly, about 10 minutes or until rice is cooked as desired. Remove from heat; stand, covered, 5 minutes.
3 Meanwhile, combine oil, chilli, rind and garlic in large bowl, add calamari; toss calamari to coat in mixture. Cook calamari on heated oiled flat plate, uncovered, until tender.
4 Divide rice and calamari among serving plates with ginger, onion, cucumber and extra chilli; serve with bowls of dipping sauce.

LEMON SOY DIPPING SAUCE Heat vinegar, sugar and sauce in small saucepan, stirring, until sugar dissolves. Remove from heat; stir in rind.

serves 4
per serving 8g fat; 2225kJ (532 cal)

asian-flavoured ocean trout with shiitake mushrooms

PREPARATION TIME 10 MINUTES **COOKING TIME** 15 MINUTES

1 tablespoon salted black
   beans, rinsed, drained
1 clove garlic, crushed
3cm piece fresh ginger
   (15g), grated
1 teaspoon dried chilli flakes
⅓ cup (80ml) soy sauce
6 green onions, sliced thinly
4 whole rainbow trout (2kg)
400g fresh shiitake mushrooms
2 tablespoons lemon juice

1 Crush beans in small bowl. Add garlic, ginger, chilli, half of the soy sauce and half of the onion; stir to combine.
2 Place each fish on oiled piece of foil large enough to completely enclose it; place a quarter of the bean mixture inside each fish, wrap tightly in foil. Cook fish on heated oiled grill plate, uncovered, about 10 minutes or until cooked as desired.
3 Meanwhile, cook mushrooms on heated oiled flat plate, uncovered, until tender; drizzle with remaining soy sauce.
4 Serve mushrooms with fish, drizzled with juice and sprinkled with remaining onion.

serves 4
per serving 10.6g fat;
1583kJ (378 cal)

mediterranean octopus salad with grilled tomatoes

PREPARATION TIME 15 MINUTES **COOKING TIME** 5 MINUTES

4 large egg tomatoes (360g),
    halved

1 tablespoon fresh
    thyme leaves

2 tablespoons olive oil

1kg cleaned baby octopus

270g jar char-grilled red
    capsicum, drained,
    sliced thinly

1 medium oak leaf lettuce, torn

2 tablespoons drained capers,
    rinsed, chopped coarsely

2 lebanese cucumbers (260g),
    chopped coarsely

½ cup (75g) seeded kalamata
    olives, chopped coarsely

½ cup coarsely chopped fresh
    flat-leaf parsley

¼ cup (60ml) lemon juice

1 clove garlic, crushed

1 Place tomato, thyme and half
   of the oil in medium bowl;
   toss gently to combine. Cook
   on heated oiled flat plate,
   uncovered, until just softened
   and browned lightly.

2 Meanwhile, cook octopus on
   heated oiled grill plate, brushing
   with remaining oil, until tender.

3 Combine remaining ingredients
   in large bowl with octopus; toss
   gently to combine. Serve salad
   with grilled tomato.

serves 4
per serving 19.4g fat;
2566kJ (613 cal)

tuna skewers with soba

PREPARATION TIME 20 MINUTES **COOKING TIME** 10 MINUTES

Searing the tuna quickly will result in fish that is somewhat rare in the middle, browned on the surface... and deliciously succulent throughout. Soak eight bamboo skewers in cold water before use to prevent them splintering or scorching.

2 tablespoons olive oil

3 teaspoons wasabi paste

1 teaspoon ground coriander

800g tuna steaks, diced into 2cm pieces

⅓ cup finely chopped fresh coriander

300g dried soba

1 medium carrot (120g), cut into matchsticks

4 green onions, sliced thickly

¼ cup firmly packed fresh coriander leaves

MIRIN DRESSING

¼ cup (60ml) mirin

2 tablespoons soy sauce

1cm piece fresh ginger (5g), grated

1 teaspoon sesame oil

1 teaspoon fish sauce

1 teaspoon sugar

1 Combine oil, wasabi and ground coriander in large bowl, add tuna; toss tuna to coat in mixture. Thread tuna onto eight skewers; sprinkle with chopped coriander.
2 Cook soba in large saucepan of boiling water, uncovered, until just tender; drain. Rinse under cold water; drain.
3 Meanwhile, make mirin dressing.
4 Combine soba in large bowl with carrot, onion, coriander leaves and half of the dressing.
5 Cook skewers on heated oiled grill plate, uncovered, until cooked as desired. Serve skewers on noodles, drizzled with remaining dressing.

MIRIN DRESSING Place ingredients in screw-top jar; shake well.

serves 4
per serving 23g fat; 2814kJ (672 cal)

prawns with pistachio potato salad

PREPARATION TIME 15 MINUTES **COOKING TIME** 15 MINUTES

1kg uncooked large
  king prawns
2 teaspoons ground cumin
2 teaspoons ground coriander
1 teaspoon hot paprika
1 clove garlic, crushed
1 lime, quartered

PISTACHIO POTATO SALAD
700g tiny new potatoes, halved
1 cup (150g) toasted shelled
  pistachios, chopped coarsely
¼ cup (60ml) lime juice
2 tablespoons olive oil
4 green onions, sliced thinly
1 medium red onion (170g),
  chopped finely

1 Shell and devein prawns, leaving
  tails intact. Combine cumin,
  coriander, paprika and garlic in
  medium bowl, add prawns; toss
  prawns to coat in mixture.
2 Make pistachio potato salad.
3 Meanwhile, cook prawns
  on heated oiled grill plate,
  uncovered, until changed in
  colour. Add lime to grill plate;
  cook until heated through.
4 Serve prawns and lime with
  pistachio potato salad.

PISTACHIO POTATO SALAD
Boil, steam or microwave potato
until tender; drain. Place potato
in large bowl with remaining
ingredients; toss to combine.

serves 4
per serving 28g fat;
2262kJ (540 cal)

blue-eye with tahini dressing and eggplant salad

PREPARATION TIME 15 MINUTES **COOKING TIME** 15 MINUTES

2 large eggplants (1kg), sliced thickly

6 blue-eye fillets (1.2g)

3 medium tomatoes (450g), seeded, sliced thickly

1 medium red capsicum (200g), sliced thickly

½ cup firmly packed fresh flat-leaf parsley leaves

¼ cup firmly packed fresh oregano leaves

2 tablespoons olive oil

¼ cup (60ml) lemon juice

2 tablespoons toasted pine nuts

TAHINI DRESSING

1 cup (280g) greek-style yogurt

½ cup (125ml) tahini

1 clove garlic, crushed

½ cup (50g) walnuts, chopped coarsely

1 small red onion (100g), chopped coarsely

1 fresh small red thai chilli, chopped coarsely

2 tablespoons lemon juice

¼ cup finely chopped fresh coriander

1 Cook eggplant on heated oiled grill plate, uncovered, until tender.

2 Meanwhile, make tahini dressing.

3 Cook fish on heated oiled grill plate, covered, until cooked as desired.

4 Place eggplant in large bowl with remaining ingredients; toss gently to combine. Serve fish with salad, dressing and lemon wedges, if desired.

TAHINI DRESSING Blend or process yogurt, tahini, garlic, nuts, onion, chilli and juice until smooth; stir in coriander.

serves 6
per serving 34.6g fat;
2146kJ (513 cal)

SEAFOOD

curried baby snapper in banana leaves

PREPARATION TIME 25 MINUTES **COOKING TIME** 20 MINUTES

2 large banana leaves
¼ cup (75g) balti curry paste
¼ cup (60ml) water
2 tablespoons lemon juice
1 teaspoon tamarind concentrate
4 whole baby snappers (1.5kg)
6cm piece fresh ginger (30g)
4 green onions, sliced thinly
1 fresh small red thai chilli, chopped finely
½ cup loosely packed fresh coriander leaves
400g tiny new potatoes, sliced thinly

1 Trim one banana leaf into four 25cm squares. Using tongs, dip one square at a time into large saucepan of boiling water; remove immediately. Rinse under cold water; pat dry with absorbent paper. Trim remaining banana leaf to fit grill plate.

2 Cook paste, stirring, in small frying pan until fragrant. Remove from heat; stir in water, juice and tamarind. Score fish both sides through thickest part of flesh, place in large shallow dish; brush both sides of fish with curry mixture.

3 Peel ginger; cut into small matchstick-size pieces; combine in small bowl with onion, chilli and coriander.

4 Place banana leaf squares on bench; divide potato slices among squares, overlapping slightly in centre of each leaf. Place one fish on potato on each leaf; top fish with equal amounts of the ginger mixture. Fold opposite corners of leaf over to cover fish; secure each parcel with kitchen string.

5 Place trimmed banana leaf on heated grill plate; place fish parcels on leaf. Cook, covered, about 20 minutes or until fish is cooked as desired and potato is tender.

serves 4
per serving 9.2g fat; 1372kJ (328 cal)

scallop and blue-eye skewers with tomato salsa

PREPARATION TIME 30 MINUTES **COOKING TIME** 10 MINUTES

Soak 12 bamboo skewers in cold water before use
to prevent them from splintering or scorching.

500g blue-eye fillets, diced into
   2cm pieces
500g scallops, roe removed
⅓ cup finely chopped fresh basil
¼ cup (60ml) red wine vinegar
2 tablespoons olive oil
1 teaspoon cracked black pepper
3 large egg tomatoes (270g),
   diced into 1cm pieces
250g yellow teardrop tomatoes,
   halved
250g cherry tomatoes, halved
½ cup loosely packed fresh
   basil leaves, torn

RED WINE VINAIGRETTE
2 tablespoons red wine vinegar
¼ cup (60ml) olive oil
1 teaspoon dijon mustard
1 teaspoon sugar

1 Thread fish and scallops,
   alternately, onto skewers; place
   in large shallow dish, drizzle
   with combined chopped basil,
   vinegar, oil and pepper.
2 Make red wine vinaigrette.
3 Cook skewers on heated oiled
   flat plate, uncovered, until
   cooked as desired.
4 Meanwhile, place tomatoes, torn
   basil and vinaigrette in medium
   bowl; toss gently to combine.
   Serve salad with skewers.

RED WINE VINAIGRETTE
Place ingredients in screw-top
jar; shake well.

serves 4
per serving 26.6g fat;
1815kJ (434 cal)

garlic prawn, capsicum and artichoke salad

PREPARATION TIME 15 MINUTES **COOKING TIME** 20 MINUTES

1kg uncooked large king prawns

4 cloves garlic, crushed

1 fresh small red thai chilli,
  chopped finely

2 tablespoons olive oil

500g small jerusalem artichokes

1 medium red capsicum (200g)

100g baby rocket leaves

CAPER DRESSING

¼ cup (60ml) lemon juice

2 tablespoons olive oil

1 tablespoon drained capers,
  rinsed, chopped finely

1 teaspoon dijon mustard

1 Shell and devein prawns, leaving tails intact. Combine garlic, chilli and half of the oil in large bowl, add prawns; toss prawns to coat in mixture.

2 Make caper dressing.

3 Scrub artichokes under water; halve lengthways. Toss artichokes with remaining oil in medium bowl; cook on heated grill plate, uncovered, until tender.

4 Meanwhile, quarter capsicums; discard seeds and membranes. Cook capsicum, uncovered, on heated oiled grill plate until tender; slice thickly.

5 Cook prawns on grill plate, uncovered, until changed in colour. Place prawns, artichokes and capsicum in large bowl with rocket and dressing; toss gently to combine.

CAPER DRESSING Place ingredients in screw-top jar; shake well.

serves 4
per serving 19.4g fat;
1322kJ (316 cal)

crab and prawn cakes with tomato remoulade

PREPARATION TIME 25 MINUTES **COOKING TIME** 15 MINUTES

200g red mullet fillets
500g fresh crab meat, chopped coarsely
1 egg white
1 fresh small red thai chilli, quartered
2cm piece fresh ginger (10g), grated
500g uncooked large king prawns, shelled, chopped coarsely
¼ cup (35g) plain flour

TOMATO REMOULADE
½ cup (150g) mayonnaise
2 teaspoons finely grated lemon rind
1 tablespoon drained capers, rinsed, chopped coarsely
2 drained anchovy fillets, chopped finely
1 fresh small red thai chilli, seeded, chopped finely
1 small tomato (90g), seeded, chopped finely
2 tablespoons finely chopped fresh flat-leaf parsley

RIBBON SALAD
2 lebanese cucumbers (260g)
2 medium carrots (240g)
3 green onions, sliced thickly
1 tablespoon lemon juice
1 tablespoon olive oil

1 Blend or process fish, crab, egg white, chilli and ginger until mixture is smooth. Stir in prawn; using hand, shape ¼-cups of the mixture into cakes. Coat cakes in flour; shake off excess flour.
2 Make tomato remoulade. Make ribbon salad.
3 Cook cakes on heated oiled flat plate, uncovered, until cooked through. Serve crab cakes with salad and remoulade.

TOMATO REMOULADE Combine ingredients in small bowl.
RIBBON SALAD Using vegetable peeler, slice cucumbers and carrots into ribbons. Place in large bowl with onion, juice and oil; toss gently to combine.

serves 4
per serving 21g fat; 1835kJ (438 cal)

mussels with beer

PREPARATION TIME 20 MINUTES **COOKING TIME** 15 MINUTES

1kg large black mussels

1 tablespoon olive oil

2 cloves garlic, crushed

1 large red onion (300g),
   sliced thinly

2 fresh long red chillies,
   seeded, sliced thinly

1½ cups (375ml) beer

2 tablespoons sweet
   chilli sauce

1 cup coarsely chopped fresh
   flat-leaf parsley

GARLIC BREAD

1 loaf turkish bread (430g)

50g butter, melted

2 cloves garlic, crushed

2 tablespoons finely chopped
   fresh flat-leaf parsley

1 Scrub mussels; remove beards.
2 Make garlic bread.
3 Meanwhile, heat oil on heated
   flat plate; cook garlic, onion and
   chilli, stirring, until onion softens.
   Add mussels and combined
   beer and chilli sauce; cook,
   covered, about 5 minutes or
   until mussels open (discard any
   that do not). Remove from heat;
   stir in parsley.
4 Serve mussels with garlic bread.

GARLIC BREAD Halve bread
horizontally; cut each half
into four pieces, brush with
combined butter, garlic and
parsley. Cook bread on heated
oiled grill plate, uncovered, until
browned both sides.

serves 4
per serving 20.5g fat;
2250kJ (537 cal)

chipotle prawns with grilled pineapple, red onion and coriander salad

PREPARATION TIME 20 MINUTES **COOKING TIME** 20 MINUTES

Chipotle is the name used for jalapeño chillies once they've been dried and smoked. Having a deep, intensely smoky flavour rather than a searing heat, chipotles are dark brown, almost black in colour and wrinkled in appearance; they are available from specialty spice stores and gourmet delicatessens.

1kg uncooked medium
  king prawns
2 medium red onions (340g),
  cut into wedges
1 small pineapple (800g),
  chopped coarsely
½ cup firmly packed fresh
  coriander leaves

CHIPOTLE PASTE
3 chipotle chillies
2 tablespoons apple cider vinegar
2 tablespoons water
1 small brown onion (80g),
  chopped coarsely
2 cloves garlic, quartered
2 teaspoons ground cumin

1 Make chipotle paste.
2 Shell and devein prawns, leaving tails intact. Combine prawns in medium bowl with half of the chipotle paste.
3 Cook onion and pineapple on heated oiled flat plate, uncovered, about 10 minutes or until just tender.
4 Cook prawns on heated oiled flat plate, uncovered, until changed in colour.
5 Combine onion and pineapple in medium bowl with coriander; serve with prawns and remaining chipotle paste.

CHIPOTLE PASTE Soak chillies in vinegar in small bowl for 10 minutes. Blend or process chilli mixture, the water, onion, garlic and cumin until smooth. Place chipotle paste in small saucepan; bring to a boil. Reduce heat; simmer, uncovered, about 10 minutes or until paste thickens.

serves 4
per serving 1g fat; 773kJ (185 cal)

corn fritters with rocket and avocado salad

PREPARATION TIME 10 MINUTES **COOKING TIME** 20 MINUTES

You need two large fresh corn cobs for this recipe.

1 cup (150g) self-raising flour
½ teaspoon bicarbonate of soda
1 cup (250ml) milk
2 eggs
2 cups (330g) fresh corn kernels
4 green onions, chopped finely
1 fresh small red thai chilli, seeded, chopped finely

TOMATO CHILLI SAUCE
425g can crushed tomatoes
1 tablespoon brown sugar
⅓ cup (80ml) sweet chilli sauce
2 tablespoons malt vinegar

ROCKET AND AVOCADO SALAD
100g baby rocket leaves
1 medium avocado (250g), sliced thinly
1 medium red onion (170g), sliced thinly
¼ cup (60ml) balsamic vinegar
1 tablespoon olive oil

1 Make tomato chilli sauce.
2 Meanwhile, sift flour and soda into medium bowl. Make well in centre of flour mixture; gradually whisk in combined milk and egg until batter is smooth. Stir corn, onion and chilli into batter.
3 Pour ¼-cup of the batter onto heated oiled flat plate; using spatula, spread batter into a round. Cook, uncovered, about 2 minutes each side or until fritter is browned lightly and cooked through, remove from flat plate; cover to keep warm. Repeat with remaining batter.
4 Meanwhile, make rocket and avocado salad.
5 Serve corn fritters with salad and sauce.

TOMATO CHILLI SAUCE Combine ingredients in medium frying pan; bring to a boil. Reduce heat; simmer, uncovered, about 10 minutes or until sauce thickens.
ROCKET AND AVOCADO SALAD Place rocket, avocado, onion and combined vinegar and oil in large bowl; toss gently to combine.

serves 4
per serving 21.8g fat; 2061kJ (492 cal)

fennel, asparagus, nashi and walnut salad

PREPARATION TIME 10 MINUTES **COOKING TIME** 20 MINUTES

6 small fennel bulbs (1.2kg),
   halved lengthways
750g asparagus, trimmed
1 tablespoon olive oil
¼ cup (60ml) walnut oil
2 teaspoons sugar
¼ cup (60ml) lemon juice
2 nashi (400g), cored
1 tablespoon finely chopped
   fresh flat-leaf parsley
½ cup (50g) toasted walnuts,
   chopped coarsely

1 Cook fennel and asparagus
   on heated oiled grill plate,
   uncovered, brushing with olive oil,
   until vegetables are just tender.
2 Meanwhile, whisk walnut oil,
   sugar and juice in large bowl.
   Cut nashi into thin wedges. Add
   fennel, nashi, parsley and nuts to
   dressing; toss gently to combine.
3 Divide asparagus among serving
   plates; top with salad.

serves 4
per serving 27.4g fat;
1487kJ (355 cal)

eggplant, fetta and capsicum stack with mesclun salad

PREPARATION TIME 15 MINUTES **COOKING TIME** 15 MINUTES

2 medium red capsicums (400g)
¼ cup (60ml) olive oil
2 tablespoons lemon juice
1 clove garlic, crushed
1 large eggplant (500g)
1 cup (150g) drained sun-dried
    tomatoes, chopped coarsely
¼ cup (50g) seeded kalamata
    olives, chopped coarsely
½ cup loosely packed fresh
    basil, torn
100g mesclun
2 tablespoons red wine vinegar
200g fetta cheese, cut into 8 slices
1 tablespoon small whole fresh
    basil leaves, extra

1   Quarter capsicums; discard seeds and
    membranes. Cook capsicum on heated
    oiled grill plate, skin-side down, until skin
    blisters and blackens. Cover with plastic
    wrap for 5 minutes; peel away skin.
2   Meanwhile, combine 2 tablespoons
    of the oil in small bowl with juice and
    garlic. Cut eggplant lengthways into
    8 slices, brush slices both sides with
    oil mixture; cook on heated oiled grill
    plate, uncovered, brushing occasionally
    with oil mixture, until just tender.
3   Combine tomato, olives and basil in
    small bowl. Place mesclun in medium
    bowl, drizzle with vinegar and
    remaining oil; toss gently to combine.
4   Place 1 slice of the eggplant on each
    serving plate; top each with 2 slices of
    the cheese, 2 pieces of the capsicum
    and 1 remaining eggplant slice. Top
    with tomato mixture, sprinkle with extra
    basil leaves; serve with salad.

serves 4
per serving 27.7g fat;
1707kJ (408 cal)

piri-piri vegetables with char-grilled polenta

PREPARATION TIME 15 MINUTES (PLUS REFRIGERATION TIME)
COOKING TIME 20 MINUTES

4 baby eggplants (240g), sliced thickly
2 medium red onions (340g), cut into wedges
2 large flat mushrooms (200g), sliced thickly
4 large egg tomatoes (360g), quartered, seeded
3 large zucchini (450g), sliced thickly lengthways
1 litre (4 cups) water
1 cup (170g) polenta
50g butter
½ cup (40g) finely grated parmesan cheese

PIRI-PIRI MARINADE
4 fresh small red thai chillies, halved
⅓ cup (80ml) red wine vinegar
2 cloves garlic, quartered
⅓ cup (80ml) olive oil

1 Make piri-piri marinade.
2 Toss eggplant, onion, mushrooms, tomato and zucchini in large bowl with marinade, cover; refrigerate overnight.
3 Meanwhile, grease deep 19cm-square cake pan. Place the water in medium saucepan; bring to a boil. Gradually add polenta to liquid, stirring constantly. Reduce heat; cook, stirring, about 10 minutes or until polenta thickens. Stir in butter and cheese then spread polenta into prepared pan; cool 10 minutes. Cover; refrigerate overnight.
4 Turn polenta onto board; trim edges. Cut polenta into quarters; cut each quarter in half diagonally to form two triangles. Cook polenta and drained vegetables on heated oiled grill plate, uncovered, about 10 minutes or until polenta is browned lightly and vegetables are tender. Serve polenta with vegetables.

PIRI-PIRI MARINADE Blend or process chilli, vinegar and garlic until smooth. With motor operating, gradually add oil in thin, steady stream until mixture thickens slightly.

serves 4
per serving 33.3g fat; 2130kJ (509 cal)

mushroom burgers with the lot

PREPARATION TIME 10 MINUTES **COOKING TIME** 15 MINUTES

In Italian, ciabatta means slipper, which is the traditional shape of this popular crisp-crusted wood-fired white bread. You can substitute it with turkish bread or focaccia if preferred.

50g baby spinach leaves
1 tablespoon lemon juice
1 tablespoon olive oil
1 teaspoon dijon mustard
4 thick slices ciabatta (200g)
1 large brown onion (200g),
  cut into 4 slices
4 large flat mushrooms (400g),
  halved
1 large tomato (220g), cut
  into 4 slices
4 eggs

1 Place spinach and combined juice, oil and mustard in medium bowl; toss gently to combine.

2 Toast ciabatta, both sides, on heated oiled grill plate; cook onion, mushrooms and tomato on same heated oiled grill plate, uncovered, until vegetables are just tender.

3 Meanwhile, cook eggs in lightly oiled egg rings on heated oiled flat plate, uncovered, until cooked as desired.

4 Divide ciabatta among serving plates; layer with mushroom, onion, tomato, egg and spinach mixture.

serves 4
per serving 11.3g fat;
1137kJ (272 cal)

grilled tofu steaks with asian vegetables

PREPARATION TIME 15 MINUTES **COOKING TIME** 15 MINUTES

600g firm tofu, sliced thickly
2 tablespoons kecap manis
2 cloves garlic, crushed
1 tablespoon sesame oil
800g baby bok choy,
   halved lengthways
200g asparagus, trimmed,
   halved lengthways
100g enoki mushrooms
6 green onions, chopped
   coarsely

GINGER DRESSING
1 tablespoon soy sauce
1 tablespoon rice vinegar
1 tablespoon oyster sauce
1cm piece fresh ginger
   (5g), grated

1 Pat tofu slices both sides with
   absorbent paper to remove
   surface liquid. Combine kecap
   manis, garlic and oil in medium
   bowl, add tofu; toss tofu gently
   to coat in mixture. Cook tofu on
   heated oiled flat plate, uncovered,
   until browned lightly both sides,
   brushing occasionally with mixture.
2 Meanwhile, make ginger dressing.
3 Cook bok choy, asparagus,
   mushrooms and onion on heated
   oiled flat plate, uncovered, until
   just tender.
4 Place vegetables in medium
   bowl, drizzle with dressing; toss
   gently to combine. Serve tofu
   with vegetables.

GINGER DRESSING Place
ingredients in screw-top jar;
shake well.

serves 4
per serving 15.4g fat;
1097kJ (262 cal)

felafel burgers

PREPARATION TIME 15 MINUTES **COOKING TIME** 10 MINUTES

A snack eaten all through the Middle-East and North Africa, felafel are small croquette-like patties made of crushed dried chickpeas or beans and a variety of herbs. They are often eaten as a vegetarian alternative to lamb in sandwiches or on mixed plates of various mezze.

2 x 300g cans chickpeas, rinsed, drained
1 medium brown onion (150g), chopped coarsely
2 cloves garlic, quartered
½ cup coarsely chopped fresh flat-leaf parsley
2 teaspoons ground coriander
1 teaspoon ground cumin
1 teaspoon bicarbonate of soda
2 tablespoons plain flour
1 egg, beaten lightly
1 loaf turkish bread (430g)
1 large tomato (220g), sliced thinly
20g rocket leaves

YOGURT AND TAHINI SAUCE
¼ cup (70g) yogurt
2 tablespoons tahini
1 tablespoon lemon juice

1 Blend or process chickpeas, onion, garlic, parsley, coriander, cumin, soda, flour and egg until almost smooth. Using hands, shape mixture into four burgers. Cook burgers on heated oiled flat plate, uncovered, about 10 minutes or until browned both sides.

2 Cut bread into quarters; toast both sides on heated oiled grill plate.

3 Meanwhile, make yogurt and tahini sauce.

4 Split each piece of bread in half horizontally; sandwich sauce, tomato, burgers and rocket between bread halves.

YOGURT AND TAHINI SAUCE Combine ingredients in small bowl.

serves 4
per serving 10.7g fat; 1989kJ (475 cal)

TIP When cooking felafel, use two spatulas to turn them carefully.

vegetable and pasta salad with sun-dried tomato mayonnaise

PREPARATION TIME 10 MINUTES **COOKING TIME** 20 MINUTES

375g penne
5 yellow patty-pan squash (150g),
    halved crossways
2 medium zucchini (240g),
    sliced thinly
350g asparagus, trimmed,
    cut into 5cm lengths
2 baby eggplants (120g),
    sliced thinly
1 small red onion (100g),
    cut into wedges
250g cherry tomatoes
1 medium red capsicum (200g),
    sliced thickly
½ cup (150g) mayonnaise
1 tablespoon sun-dried
    tomato pesto

1 Cook pasta in large saucepan
   of boiling water, uncovered,
   until just tender; drain.
2 Meanwhile, cook vegetables
   on heated oiled grill plate,
   uncovered, until just tender.
3 Combine mayonnaise and
   pesto in large bowl. Add
   pasta and vegetables; toss
   gently to combine.

serves 4
per serving 15.5g fat;
2225kJ (531 cal)

pumpkin and haloumi salad

PREPARATION TIME 15 MINUTES **COOKING TIME** 10 MINUTES

650g pumpkin, cut into
   thin wedges
200g green beans, halved
2 tablespoons olive oil
2 tablespoons red wine vinegar
¾ cup loosely packed fresh
   coriander leaves
¾ cup loosely packed fresh
   flat-leaf parsley leaves
100g baby spinach leaves
⅓ cup (55g) toasted pepitas
250g haloumi cheese,
   sliced thickly

1 Boil, steam or microwave
   pumpkin and beans, separately,
   until almost tender; drain. Rinse
   under cold water; drain. Place
   pumpkin on heated oiled grill
   plate; cook, uncovered, until
   wedges are tender.
2 Meanwhile, place oil, vinegar,
   coriander, parsley, spinach and
   pepitas in large bowl; toss gently
   to combine.
3 Cook cheese on heated oiled
   grill plate, uncovered, until
   browned both sides. Add
   cheese, pumpkin and beans
   to bowl with spinach mix; toss
   gently to combine.

serves 4
per serving 27.4g fat;
1645kJ (393 cal)

barbecued fetta on greek salad

PREPARATION TIME 15 MINUTES **COOKING TIME** 5 MINUTES

4 x 100g pieces fetta cheese
2 teaspoons finely chopped fresh oregano
2 teaspoons finely chopped fresh marjoram
2 cloves garlic, chopped finely
1 tablespoon olive oil
4 thick slices sourdough bread (160g)
100g baby spinach leaves
¾ cup (110g) seeded kalamata olives
⅔ cup (100g) drained semi-dried tomatoes
12 drained marinated quartered artichoke hearts (150g)
⅔ cup (110g) drained caperberries, rinsed
2 tablespoons lemon juice

1 Place each piece of cheese on a 20cm-square piece of foil; using fingers, rub combined herbs, garlic and oil gently into cheese. Wrap foil around cheese to enclose.
2 Place foil parcels on heated grill plate; cook, uncovered, about 5 minutes or until cheese is heated through. Toast bread both sides on heated oiled grill plate.
3 Meanwhile, place spinach, olives, tomato, artichokes, caperberries and juice in large bowl; toss gently to combine.
4 Divide salad among serving plates; top with bread and cheese.

serves 4
per serving 32g fat; 2305kJ (551 cal)

soya bean and potato patties with teardrop tomato salsa

PREPARATION TIME 20 MINUTES **COOKING TIME** 20 MINUTES

700g potatoes,
   chopped coarsely

4 green onions, sliced thinly

1 clove garlic, crushed

300g can soya beans,
   rinsed, drained

1 teaspoon ground cumin

½ cup (60g) coarsely grated
   cheddar cheese

1 tablespoon plain flour

TEARDROP TOMATO SALSA

500g yellow teardrop
   tomatoes, halved

⅓ cup finely chopped
   fresh coriander

1 small red onion (100g),
   chopped finely

1 fresh long red chilli, seeded,
   sliced thinly

1 tablespoon red wine vinegar

1 tablespoon lime juice

1 tablespoon olive oil

1 Boil, steam or microwave potato until tender; drain.

2 Meanwhile, make teardrop tomato salsa.

3 Coarsely mash potato in large bowl. Stir in remaining ingredients; using hands, shape mixture into eight patties. Cook patties on heated oiled flat plate, uncovered, until heated through. Serve patties with salsa.

TEARDROP TOMATO SALSA

Place ingredients in medium bowl; toss gently to combine.

serves 4
per serving 12.8g fat;
1188kJ (284 cal)

turkish bread vegetable pizza

PREPARATION TIME 15 MINUTES **COOKING TIME** 20 MINUTES

1 medium zucchini (120g),
  sliced thinly
2 baby eggplants (120g),
  sliced thinly
1 small kumara (250g),
  sliced thinly
1 medium red capsicum (200g),
  sliced thickly
200g mushrooms, sliced thickly
1 loaf turkish bread (430g)
⅓ cup (85g) bottled tomato
  pasta sauce
¼ cup (65g) sun-dried
  tomato pesto
125g cherry tomatoes, quartered
⅔ cup (100g) seeded
  kalamata olives
1¼ cups (125g) coarsely grated
  mozzarella cheese

1 Cook zucchini, eggplant, kumara,
  capsicum and mushrooms on
  heated oiled flat plate, uncovered,
  until tender.
2 Cut bread into quarters; split
  each piece in half horizontally.
  Brush cut-side of each bread
  piece with combined pasta
  sauce and pesto. Divide grilled
  vegetables, tomato, olives and
  cheese among bread pieces.
3 Cook pizzas on heated oiled flat
  plate, covered, until bases are
  crisp and cheese melts.

serves 4
per serving 18.4g fat;
2302kJ (550 cal)

vegetarian skewers

PREPARATION TIME 10 MINUTES **COOKING TIME** 10 MINUTES

Bocconcini, which translates from Italian as "little mouthfuls", are delectably creamy balls of fresh mozzarella originally used in salads such as the caprese, but today eaten in all sorts of dishes all around the world. It is available in two sizes, one about as big as a walnut and the other (which we used here) even smaller, commonly referred to as cherry bocconcini. For this recipe, you need to soak 12 bamboo skewers in cold water before use to prevent them splintering or scorching.

2 tablespoons sun-dried tomato pesto
¼ cup (60ml) lemon juice
2 tablespoons olive oil
1 small red onion (100g), quartered
1 small green capsicum (150g), chopped coarsely
6 vegetarian sausages (300g), sliced thickly
250g cherry tomatoes, halved
100g ciabatta, diced into 2cm pieces
8 cherry bocconcini (80g)

1 Combine pesto, juice and oil in small bowl.
2 Thread onion, capsicum, sausage and half of the tomato, alternately, onto eight skewers. Thread bread, cheese and remaining tomato, alternately, onto four skewers.
3 Brush skewers with pesto mixture; cook on heated oiled grill plate, uncovered, brushing occasionally with pesto mixture, until skewers are browned lightly. Divide skewers among serving plates; drizzle with remaining pesto mixture.

serves 4
per serving 22.4g fat; 1515kJ (362 cal)

ABOUT BARBECUING

The backyard barbie has come a long way from the time when dad donned an apron and charred the sausages. Today, it has become an indispensable part of summer life and, in many cases, thanks to gas and electric barbecues, a regular cooking regimen for those people who barbecue several nights of the week. And why not? Barbecuing keeps the kitchen clean, uses fewer pans and helps make washing up a breeze.

CHOOSING THE BARBECUE

Barbecues come in two types: covered (also known as kettle barbecues) and uncovered. A covered barbecue is the most practical because you can use it as an oven with the cover closed, or as a traditional barbecue with the cover open. Small covered barbecues can be used on terraces or balconies. However, if you normally entertain on a large scale, you probably need a big fixed barbecue. If you only use your barbecue for quickly cooking steaks, chops, fish and sausages, a simple portable barbecue with no cover could suit your requirements perfectly.

CLEANING THE BARBECUE

All barbecues should be cleaned after use. It's much easier to clean a still-warm barbecue than a cold, food-encrusted one. A gas barbecue should be turned onto high and, when the grill plate starts to smoke, should first be turned off at the bottle to prevent gas build-up in the hose, then at the controls.

For all types of barbecues, use a stiff wire brush and cold water (no detergent) to scrub the grill and plate. Lightly spray or brush the grill with vegetable oil before putting it away to help prevent it rusting. If your barbecue can't be moved out of the rain, invest in a vinyl cover to protect it from rust.

Ash from wood or charcoal barbecues should be cooled completely and then, if you like, spread evenly over your garden. If you have a small garden, and barbecue frequently, this clearly will not be a long-term solution so you'll have to resort to placing the cooled ash in a plastic bag then discarding it.

THE FUEL

Barbecues can be fuelled by wood, charcoal and heat beads, gas or electricity. Wood requires pieces of various sizes, kindling and paper. Allow wood to char before cooking and never use treated wood on a barbecue. Move food away from extreme heat to prevent burning. Charcoal is made from hardwood or lumpwood. It lights quickly, burns with twice the heat of beads and smells cleaner. Heat beads or briquettes are made from ground charcoal, coal dust and starch. For direct cooking, one layer of charcoal or heat beads should cover an area slightly larger than the food. For indirect cooking, use twice the depth of coals as they have to burn longer. Place charcoal or heat beads in a mound and insert two or three firelighters among them. Don't attempt to cook anything while the firelighters are burning or your food will taste of kerosene. Allow the coals to burn until they're covered with grey ash (about 30 minutes) then spread them out before you start cooking. To increase heat, tap coals with metal tongs to remove accumulated ash then push them closer together; open all vents and add more charcoal. To make the heat less intense, partially close all the vents and push the coals further apart.

Gas or electric barbecues are faster and heat in about 15 minutes. Gas barbecues come with an empty gas bottle; electric barbecues require a nearby power source. Most models have heat controls and at least two burners so you can cook various foods simultaneously. Gas barbecues have a slide-out draining tray, which should be lined with foil and sprinkled evenly with fat absorber. Fit a gas-fuse between the cylinder bottle and the regulator to prevent gas leaks and possible disastrous explosions.

glossary

ALLSPICE also known as pimento or jamaican pepper; so-named because it tastes like a combination of nutmeg, cumin, cinnamon and clove. Is available whole (a pea-sized dark-brown berry) or ground, and used in both sweet and savoury dishes.

AMERICAN-STYLE PORK SPARERIBS trimmed, long mid-loin ribs.

ARTICHOKE
globe large flower-bud of a member of the thistle family; having tough petal-like leaves, edible in part when cooked.
hearts tender centre of the globe artichoke. Artichoke hearts can be harvested fresh from the plant or purchased in brine canned or in glass jars.
jerusalem neither from Jerusalem nor an artichoke, this crunchy tuber tastes a bit like a fresh water chestnut and is related to the sunflower family.

BACON RASHERS also known as slices of bacon, made from pork side, cured and smoked. Middle rashers are the familiar bacon shape, ie, a thin strip of belly pork having a lean, rather round piece of loin at one end.

BOK CHOY also called pak choi or chinese white cabbage; has a fresh, mild mustard taste and is good braised or in stir-fries. Baby bok choy is also available and is slightly more tender than bok choy.

BUTTER use salted or unsalted ("sweet") butter; 125g is equal to one stick of butter.

CAPSICUM also known as bell pepper or, simply, pepper. Native to Central and South America, capsicums come in many colours: red, green, yellow, orange and purplish-black. Be sure to discard seeds and membranes before use.

CELERIAC tuberous root with brown skin, white flesh and a celery-like flavour; can be grated and eaten raw in salads or cooked like potato and mashed.

CHEESE
bocconcini from the diminutive of boccone meaning mouthful, is the term used for walnut-sized baby mozzarella, a delicate, semi-soft, white cheese traditionally made in Italy from buffalo milk. Spoils rapidly so must be kept under refrigeration, in brine, for one or two days at most.
haloumi a firm, cream-coloured sheep-milk cheese matured in brine; somewhat like a minty, salty fetta in flavour, haloumi can be grilled or fried, briefly, without breaking down.
pizza a commercial blend of varying proportions of processed grated cheddar, mozzarella and parmesan.
provolone an Italian cheese that is mild when young, similar to mozzarella. Golden yellow in colour, with a smooth shiny skin.

CHAR SUI SAUCE sometimes called chinese barbecue sauce, this paste-like ingredient is a dark-red-brown in colour and sweet and spicy in flavour. Made with fermented soybeans, honey and various spices.

CHERVIL also known as cicily; fennel-flavoured herb with minuscule curly dark-green leaves.

CHILLI generally the smaller the chilli, the hotter it is. Use rubber gloves when seeding and chopping fresh chillies to prevent burning your skin.

CHINESE RICE WINE a clear distillation of fermented rice, water and salt, about 29.5% alcohol by volume; used for marinades and as a sauce ingredient.

CHOY SUM also known as pakaukeo or flowering cabbage, a member of the bok choy family; easy to identify with its long stems, light green leaves and yellow flowers. Is eaten, stems and all, steamed or stir-fried.

CORIANDER also known as cilantro or chinese parsley; bright-green leafy herb with a pungent flavour. Also sold as seeds, whole or ground.

CORNFLOUR also known as cornstarch; used as a thickening agent in all types of cooking.

COS LETTUCE also known as romaine lettuce; the traditional Caesar salad lettuce having pale green, long tapering leaves.

COUSCOUS a fine, grain-like cereal product, originally from North Africa; made from semolina.

CRAISINS dried cranberries.

EGG some recipes call for raw or barely cooked eggs; exercise caution if there's a salmonella problem in your area.

FISH SAUCE also called nam pla or nuoc nam; made from pulverised, salted, fermented fish, most often anchovies. Has a pungent smell and strong taste; use sparingly.

FIVE-SPICE POWDER fragrant ground mixture of cinnamon, clove, star anise, sichuan pepper and fennel seeds.

FLOUR, PLAIN an all-purpose flour, made from wheat.

GARAM MASALA a blend of spices based on varying proportions of cardamom, cloves, cinnamon, coriander, fennel and cumin, roasted and then ground together.

GINGER also known as green or root ginger; the thick root of a tropical plant. Pickled ginger is sold in pieces or sliced; comes in red and pink varieties packed in a seasoned brine.

GREEN ONION also known as scallion or (incorrectly) shallot; an immature onion picked before the bulb has formed, having a long, bright-green edible stalk.

HOISIN SAUCE a thick sweet and spicy Chinese paste made from salted fermented soy beans, onions, garlic and various spices; used as a marinade or baste, or to accent stir-fries and barbecued or roasted foods.

HUMMUS a Middle-Eastern salad or dip made from softened dried chickpeas, garlic, lemon juice and tahini (sesame seed paste); can be purchased, ready-made, from supermarkets.

KALONJI also known as nigella seeds; angular seeds that are black on the outside and creamy within, and have a sharp, nutty flavour. They can be found in specialty spice shops and all Asian food stores.

KECAP MANIS also known as ketjap manis; a thick soy sauce with added sugar and spices.

KIPFLER POTATO small, finger-shaped potato having a nutty flavour.

KUMARA Polynesian name of orange-fleshed sweet potato, often confused with yam.

LAVASH also known as mountain bread; a flat, unleavened bread of Mediterranean origin.

LEBANESE CUCUMBER short, thin-skinned and slender; also known as the european cucumber.

MINCE also known as ground meat.

MIRIN sweet rice wine used in Japanese cooking; not to be confused with sake.

MIZUNA a wispy, green salad leaf that originated in Japan.

MUSHROOMS

flat large, flat mushrooms with a rich earthy flavour. They are sometimes misnamed field mushrooms which are wild mushrooms.

shiitake when fresh are also known as chinese black, forest or golden oak mushrooms; although cultivated, have the earthiness and taste of wild mushrooms. Are large and meaty; often used as a substitute for meat in some Asian vegetarian dishes. When dried, they are known as donko or dried chinese mushrooms; rehydrate before use.

swiss brown light- to dark-brown mushrooms with full-bodied flavour; also known as roman or cremini. Button or cap mushrooms can be substituted.

NAAN round leavened bread associated with the tandoori dishes of northern India; there, it is baked pressed against the inside wall of a heated tandoor or clay oven.

NOODLES

fried noodles also known as crispy noodles and used in chow mein and sang choy bow; packaged (commonly in 100g packets) already deep-fried.

hokkien also known as stir-fry noodles; fresh wheat noodles resembling thick, yellow-brown spaghetti needing no pre-cooking before being used.

rice soft white noodles made from rice flour and vegetable oil; available in varying thicknesses, from vermicelli-thin to broad and flat. Rinse under hot water to remove starch and excess oil before using.

PAPAYA, GREEN readily available in various sizes at many Asian shops and markets; look for one that is very hard and slightly shiny, which indicates that it is freshly picked.

PITTA also known as Lebanese bread. This wheat-flour pocket bread is sold in large, flat pieces that separate into two thin rounds. Also available in small thick pieces called pocket pitta.

POLENTA also known as cornmeal; a flour-like cereal made of dried corn (maize) sold ground in different textures; also the name of the dish made from it.

PRESERVED LEMON a North African speciality, the citrus is preserved, usually whole, in a mixture of salt and lemon juice. Can be rinsed and eaten as is, or added to casseroles and tagines to impart a rich salty-sour acidic flavour.

PROSCIUTTO cured, air-dried, pressed ham; usually sold thinly sliced.

QUINCE yellow-skinned fruit with hard texture and astringent, tart taste; eaten cooked or as a preserve.

SAKE rice wine used in cooking or as a drink. If unavailable, substitute dry sherry or brandy.

SAMBAL OELEK (also ulek or olek) Indonesian in origin; a salty paste made from ground chillies.

SHALLOT also called french shallot, golden shallot or eschalot; small, brown-skinned, elongated member of the onion family. Grows in tight clusters similarly to garlic.

SICHUAN PEPPERCORNS also known as szechuan or chinese pepper. Not related to the peppercorn family, small, red-brown berries look like peppercorns and have a peppery-lemon flavour.

SILVERBEET also known as swiss chard or chard; a leafy, dark-green vegetable, related to the beet, with thick, crisp white or red stems and ribs. The leaves, often trimmed from the stems and ribs, are used raw or cooked.

STAR ANISE a dried star-shaped pod that has an astringent aniseed flavour; used to flavour stocks and marinades.

SUGAR

caster also known as superfine or finely granulated table sugar.

palm also known as nam tan pip, jaggery, jawa or gula melaka; made from the sap of the sugar palm tree. Light brown to black in colour and usually sold in rock-hard cakes; substitute it with brown sugar if unavailable.

SUGAR SNAP PEAS also known as honey snap peas; fresh small pea which can be eaten, whole, pod and all, similarly to snow peas.

SUMAC a purple-red, astringent spice ground from berries growing on shrubs that flourish wild around the Mediterranean; adds a tart, lemony flavour to dips and dressings and goes well with barbecued meat. Can be found in Middle-Eastern food stores.

TAHINI sesame seed paste available from Middle-Eastern food stores; most often used in hummus, baba ghanoush and other Lebanese recipes.

TAMARI a thick, dark soy sauce made mainly from soy beans without the wheat used in standard soy sauce.

TAMARIND, concentrate the commercial distillation of tamarind pulp into a condensed paste. Used straight from the container, with no soaking or straining required; can be diluted with water according to taste.

TAPENADE a thick, black paste made from black olives, olive oil, capers, anchovies and Mediterranean herbs.

TAT SOI also known as rosette, pak choy, tai gu choy and chinese flat cabbage; a variety of bok choy. Its dark green leaves are cut into sections rather than separated.

THAI BASIL has smallish leaves, and sweet licorice/aniseed taste; it is one of the basic flavours that typify Thai cuisine. Available in Asian supermarkets and greengrocers.

TURKISH BREAD also known as pide. Comes in long (about 45cm) flat loaves as well as individual rounds; made from wheat flour and sprinkled with sesame or black onion seeds.

TURMERIC a rhizome related to galangal and ginger; must be grated or pounded to release its somewhat acrid aroma and pungent flavour.

WITLOF sometimes spelled witloof, and in some countries known as belgian endive or chicory, witlof is a versatile vegetable as good eaten cooked as it is raw.

ZA'ATAR a dry blend of roasted sesame seeds, wild marjoram, thyme and sumac available from Middle-Eastern specialty food shops.

ZUCCHINI also known as courgette; a small green, yellow or white vegetable belonging to the squash family.

index

facts + figures

Wherever you live, you'll be able to use our recipes with the help of these easy-to-follow conversions. While these conversions are approximate only, the difference between an exact and the approximate conversion of various liquid and dry measures is but minimal, and will not affect your cooking results.

dry measures

metric	imperial
15g	½oz
30g	1oz
60g	2oz
90g	3oz
125g	4oz (¼lb)
155g	5oz
185g	6oz
220g	7oz
250g	8oz (½lb)
280g	9oz
315g	10oz
345g	11oz
375g	12oz (¾lb)
410g	13oz
440g	14oz
470g	15oz
500g	16oz (1lb)
750g	24oz (1½lb)
1kg	32oz (2lb)

liquid measures

metric	imperial
30ml	1 fluid oz
60ml	2 fluid oz
100ml	3 fluid oz
125ml	4 fluid oz
150ml	5 fluid oz (¼ pint/1 gill)
190ml	6 fluid oz
250ml	8 fluid oz
300ml	10 fluid oz (½ pint)
500ml	16 fluid oz
600ml	20 fluid oz (1 pint)
1000ml (1 litre)	1¾ pints

helpful measures

metric	imperial
3mm	⅛in
6mm	¼in
1cm	½in
2cm	¾in
2.5cm	1in
5cm	2in
6cm	2½in
8cm	3in
10cm	4in
13cm	5in
15cm	6in
18cm	7in
20cm	8in
23cm	9in
25cm	10in
28cm	11in
30cm	12in (1ft)

measuring equipment

The difference between one country's measuring cups and another's is, at most, within a 2 or 3 teaspoon variance. (For the record, one Australian metric measuring cup holds approximately 250ml.) The most accurate way of measuring dry ingredients is to weigh them. When measuring liquids, use a clear glass or plastic jug with metric markings. (For the record, one Australian metric tablespoon holds 20ml; one Australian metric teaspoon holds 5ml.)

Note: NZ, Canada, US and UK use 15ml tablespoons. All cup and spoon measurements are level.

We use large eggs with an average weight of 60g.

how to measure

When using graduated metric measuring cups, shake dry ingredients loosely into the appropriate cup. Do not tap the cup on a bench or tightly pack the ingredients unless directed to do so. Level top of measuring cups and measuring spoons with a knife. When measuring liquids, place a clear glass or plastic jug with metric markings on a flat surface to check accuracy at eye level.

oven temperatures

These oven temperatures are only a guide. Always check the manufacturer's manual.

	°C (Celsius)	°F (Fahrenheit)	Gas Mark
Very slow	120	250	½
Slow	140 – 150	275 – 300	1 – 2
Moderately slow	170	325	3
Moderate	180 – 190	350 – 375	4 – 5
Moderately hot	200	400	6
Hot	220 – 230	425 – 450	7 – 8
Very hot	240	475	9

Looking after **your interest...**

Keep your ACP cookbooks clean, tidy and within easy reach with slipcovers designed to hold up to 12 books. Plus you can follow our recipes perfectly with a set of accurate measuring cups and spoons, as used by *The Australian Women's Weekly* Test Kitchen.

To order

Mail or fax Photocopy and complete the coupon below and post to ACP Books Reader Offer, ACP Publishing, GPO Box 4967, Sydney NSW 2001, or fax to (02) 9267 4967.

Phone Have your credit card details ready, then phone 136 116 (Mon-Fri, 8.00am-6.00pm; Sat, 8.00am-6.00pm).

Price

Book Holder

Australia: $13.10 (incl. GST).
Elsewhere: $A21.95.

Metric Measuring Set

Australia: $6.50 (incl. GST).
New Zealand: $A8.00.
Elsewhere: $A9.95.

Prices include postage and handling. This offer is available in all countries.

Payment

Australian residents

We accept the credit cards listed on the coupon, money orders and cheques.

Overseas residents

We accept the credit cards listed on the coupon, drafts in $A drawn on an Australian bank, and also UK, NZ and US cheques in the currency of the country of issue. Credit card charges are at the exchange rate current at the time of payment.

Test Kitchen
Food director *Pamela Clark*
Food editor *Karen Hammial*
Assistant food editor *Amira Georgy*
Test kitchen managers Kimberley Coverdale,
 Cathie Lonnie
Home economists *Sammie Coryton,*
 Nancy Duran, Elizabeth Macri,
 Christina Martignago, Sharon Reeve,
 Susie Riggall, Kirrily Smith
Editorial coordinator *Rebecca Steyns*
Nutritional information *Laila Ibram*

ACP Books
Editorial director *Susan Tomnay*
Creative director *Hieu Chi Nguyen*
Senior editor *Wendy Bryant*
Designer *Mary Keep*
Studio manager *Caryl Wiggins*
Editorial/sales coordinator *Caroline Lowry*
Editorial assistant *Karen Lai*
Publishing manager (sales) *Brian Cearnes*
Publishing manager (rights & new projects)
 Jane Hazell
Marketing manager *Sarah Cave*
Pre-press *Harry Palmer*
Production manager *Carol Currie*
Business manager *Seymour Cohen*
Assistant business analyst *Martin Howes*
Chief executive officer *John Alexander*
Group publisher *Pat Ingram*
Publisher *Sue Wannan*
Editor-in-chief *Deborah Thomas*
Produced by ACP Books, Sydney.
Printed by Dai Nippon Printing in Korea.
Published by ACP Publishing Pty Limited, 54 Park St, Sydney; GPO Box 4088, Sydney, NSW 2001.
Ph: (02) 9282 8618 Fax: (02) 9267 9438.
www.acpbooks.com.au
To order books, phone 136 116.
Send recipe enquiries to:
recipeenquiries@acp.com.au
AUSTRALIA: Distributed by Network Services, GPO Box 4088, Sydney, NSW 2001.
Ph: (02) 9282 8777 Fax: (02) 9264 3278.
UNITED KINGDOM: Distributed by Australian Consolidated Press (UK), Moulton Park Business Centre, Red House Rd, Moulton Park, Northampton, NN3 6AQ.
Ph: (01604) 497 531 Fax: (01604) 497 533
acpukltd@aol.com
CANADA: Distributed by Whitecap Books Ltd, 351 Lynn Ave, North Vancouver, BC, V7J 2C4.
Ph: (604) 980 9852 Fax: (604) 980 8197
customerservice@whitecap.ca
www.whitecap.ca
NEW ZEALAND: Distributed by Netlink Distribution Company, ACP Media Centre, Cnr Fanshawe and Beaumont Streets, Westhaven, Auckland.
PO Box 47906, Ponsonby, Auckland, NZ.
Ph: (09) 366 9966 ask@ndcnz.co.nz

Clark, Pamela.
The Australian Women's Weekly barbecue meals in minutes

Includes index.
ISBN 1 86396 365 0
1. Barbecue cookery. 2. Quick and easy cookery. I Australian Women's Weekly. II Title

641.5784

© ACP Publishing Pty Limited 2004
ABN 18 053 273 546

Photocopy and complete coupon below

☐ **Book Holder**

☐ **Metric Measuring Set**
  Please indicate number(s) required.

Mr/Mrs/Ms _____

Address _____

_____

Postcode _____ Country _____

Ph: Business hours (   ) _____

I enclose my cheque/money order for $ _____ payable to ACP Publishing.

OR: please charge my

☐ Bankcard ☐ Visa ☐ Mastercard

☐ Diners Club ☐ American Express

| | | | | | | | | | | | | | | | | |

Card number

Expiry date ____ / ____

Cardholder's signature _____

Please allow up to 30 days delivery within Australia.
Allow up to 6 weeks for overseas deliveries.
Both offers expire 31/12/05. HLBMIM05